Combat Boots to Internet Entrepreneur

Breaching The Wall

A Soldier's Story of Life as an Entrepreneur.
How You can "Breach the Wall" Yourself from
Employee to Entrepreneur!

Jason T. Miller

FIRST EDITION

ISBN: 978-1-957217-07-9 (paperback)
ISBN: 978-1-957217-08-6 (hardback)
ISBN: 978-1-957217-09-3 (ebook)

CONTENTS

Famous Quotes about Entrepreneurship

"Your time is limited, so don't waste it living someone else's life. Don't be trapped by dogma -- which is living with the results of other people's thinking. Don't let the noise of other's opinions drown out your own inner voice. And most important, have the courage to follow your heart and intuition. They somehow already know what you truly want to become. Everything else is secondary."

-- Steve Jobs, Co-founder, CEO, Chairman Apple Inc.

"Every time you state what you want or believe, you're the first to hear it. It's a message to both you and others about what you think is possible. Don't put a ceiling on yourself."

-- Oprah Winfrey, media proprietor

"Don't be afraid to assert yourself, have confidence in your abilities and don't let the bastards get you down."

-- Michael Bloomberg, founder Bloomberg L.P.

DEDICATION

This book is dedicated to all aspiring entrepreneurs that are, "Breaching the Wall" within their own lives, and was designed to help those that are willing to step outside their comfort zone and become the CEO of their own lives.

I would further like to dedicate this book to the military members and family members (my brothers and sisters) that have paid the ultimate sacrifice. The world is forever in your debt.

I wrote this book to bring forward new possibilities in your life as an entrepreneur. I want to give you the encouragement, tips, tricks and strategies I have used as an entrepreneur. I encourage you to think big and allow your creative imagination to skyrocket you to new heights in your life.

"Risk more than others think is safe. Dream more than others think is practical."

--Howard Schultz, Starbucks CEO

ACKNOWLEDGEMENT

I would like to personally thank my mentors that have helped me make this book possible and have influenced my decision-making process as an entrepreneur. I appreciate each of you and you know exactly who you are. Thank you for the valuable time, input and feedback that you have provided me as a business owner and entrepreneur. Without your guidance, counsel and occasional tough love, our business would not be where it is today.

My family is forever in your debt and we appreciate you very much!

SPECIAL SHOUT OUTS

To my wife Erika -- I wouldn't be where I am without you... You are a very special woman and I love you!

To the men of 101st ABN DIV, HHC 3-327th Infantry Recon Platoon.... I salute you!

To my ultimate mentor and great friend T.J. Rohleder -- You have been an inspiration and the best mentor one could ever ask for. Thank you for writing the forward in this book.

To my family -- All of you have influenced my life in one way or another. Specifically my father Terry. Thanks for raising me tough and resilient and being there for me.

To my friends and mentors Tom Still and Dr. Kevin Williams -- Thank you for your words of wisdom and helping me title and edit this book!

FOREWORD

Can __This__ Book Change Your Life?

THE ANSWER WILL SURPRISE YOU!

The Greek Shipbuilder Aristotle Onassis once said; "the secret to getting rich is to know something that nobody else knows."

This quote is perfect for this book. Why? Because when it comes to making a lot of money, the author, Jason T. Miller truly does know what nobody else knows. From the first time I met him and his wife Erika at a mastermind meeting in the Dominican Republic, I knew there was something special about him. He told me he joined the Army when he was 17 and was getting ready to retire, but wasn't ready to retire! He told me what he's about to tell you; that he is on a mission to take all of the principles he mastered during his highly successful military career and teach others how to use them to make money.

He made the bold statement that he had dedicated his life to helping millions of people become successfully self-employed.

"Can this be true?"

"Was he really serious?"

"Could he really pull this off?"

I was skeptical but very curious!

So I stayed in touch with him. He seemed like such an amazing guy and I loved the way that he and Erika worked together. I immediately got the feeling that they were so much different than most of the young entrepreneurs I meet. I could sense that they are such an amazing couple, and I was right! The more I knew about them, the more I was convinced that they are the REAL DEAL! As the months rolled on, I kept saying: "I want to be on their team!" I wanted to see how much money we could make together.

NOW YOU CAN JOIN THEM, TOO!

Read Jason's story. You'll see; he is a true leader who practices what he preaches! He is disciplined, motivated and focused on doing all he can to help as many others as possible. And he's learned many things about what it takes to make the largest amount of money. Now he'll take you, step-by-step, into the same process that he and Erika are using every day.

In this book, Jason will show you exactly what you must do to make the largest amount of money in the fastest and for the longest period of time. You'll be cashing in with the best-of-the-best of everything that he and Erika are doing to build their own highly successful business. As you'll see; Jason's methods work like magic!

EVERYTHING YOU NEED IS HERE

I have researched and investigated thousands of money making and business opportunities since 1988, and I've grown quite skeptical and even a bit cynical. As you may know; the business opportunity market is filled with many dishonest people who make a lot of big and bold promises that turn out to be lies. I have been lied to and cheated and misled so many times by so many people that I don't believe anyone in the beginning... So there I am, the night before I left the Dominican Republic and I'm listening to Jason Miller tell me how he's setting out to help millions of people become successfully self-employed. I looked in his eyes and knew he was serious. I was deeply impressed, but I'm still a skeptic...

However, the more time I've spent with Jason, the more I knew for a fact that he is so much different than all of the other 'big dreamers' I meet. He has the vision. But he also has the extreme discipline, motivation and focus to make it happen. So I guess I'm not a total cynic after all! I am very skeptical and you should be, too. But I'm at least willing to take a fair look at what a person has to offer ... And the longer I know Jason, the more I had to know his secrets. So after knowing him for a substantial period of time, **I was thrilled when he sent me this book you're holding in your hands!** Because I've been self-employed for over 30-years, I thought I knew almost everything about what it takes to make money, but I was wrong! I have learned many things in this book. You will, too!

Jason loves to share his best information. He loves to help people succeed. In fact, that's one of his greatest secrets. He is a true leader who cares about helping others. Prospective buyers sense this about him and want to do business with him. That's a big part of his magic. Of course, I'm simplifying all of this. There's much more to his phenomenal success than just being a super nice guy who wants to help people succeed in the biggest way... After all, there's a lot of nice people, but what's truly rare are nice people who know how to make massive sums of money.

And that's what Jason Miller is all about. The man is truly different. So are the methods and strategies he will teach you.

Read this book carefully. Prove this to yourself. And don't let the size of it fool you. Although this is not a big book, it contains some very big and powerful tips, tricks and strategies that he and his joint venture partners are using to become financially set for life. Now you can be one of these people!

THE SECRET

The secret to making money is very simple: find somebody who is already achieving great success. Get them to give you ALL of their secrets. Then do what they are doing. For best results, whenever you have any questions or need help, just contact them. That's it. But how realistic is this? Is it even possible? In most cases, you know the answer: 'NO WAY!' In most situations, when somebody has a proven way to make a ton of money they either keep it to themselves, or only share it with their best friends. That's why the rich keep getting richer; they keep their greatest money making secrets to themselves. That's the way the world works. But not anymore. Because as you'll see; Jason Miller not only freely shares his greatest tips, tricks and powerful money-making strategies, but he offers to help you every step of the way. And these are little known secrets that almost nobody knows. Those who do are making a lot of money. You're about to be one of these people. So read on and start cashing in with these little known methods. Then let Jason and Erika do their best to help you make all the money you want, need and truly deserve!

Sincerely,

T.J. Rohleder

T.J. Rohleder aka; 'The Blue Jeans Millionaire' *
www.TJRohleder.com

Why You Are Reading This Book

What is your why? Do you know why you are here right now in this moment reading this book? I can make an educated guess as to why. You are most likely at a point in time in your life just as I was. You are either transitioning from a job, getting out of the military or you're completely fed up with your current situation in life. Regardless of the specifics, the bottom line is you're here with this book in your hand for a reason. Right here and right now will determine the next course of your ultimate destiny.

I hope you choose to read every page of this book and make the best possible use of it in your search for whatever it is you are seeking in your life. A good friend and mentor once told me that we spend our whole life doing things to make other people or companies successful. At the very core of our existence we are human beings not human doings. I encourage you to find your niche and place in the world. You're here because you want to follow your passion in life and you aspire to be more than just a doer of things.

You should strive to be the CEO of your own life and be the human being that you were meant to be in this world. You are also here because you are seeking change in your life. Finding that change revolves around meeting the right people at the right time that will help you reach the aspirations that you want to reach in your life. Consider this book as a short roadmap to help you discover yourself and discover ways to take your aspirations from an idea to your ultimate reality.

BREACHING THE WALL YOURSELF

B y the time you finish reading this book you will have the tools to, "Breach the Wall" yourself. This is a mindset shift that I had to make after 22 years in the military and being "conditioned" as an employee. It will become evident to you at some point that you can do this yourself. Face your fears and don't let the unknown be your enemy. You can do anything you set your mind, energy and passion to with the right tools and mentorship to assist you along the way.

This is the essence of being able to "Breach the Wall" yourself as someone who aspires for the freedom to live an entrepreneurial life. In this book, I will share many avenues and models that you can implement yourself to "Breach the Wall" and start living the dream that you wish to achieve in your life. It will take hard work, dedication and blood sweat and tears, but at the end of it all you will stand proud knowing that you created something more for yourself and your family if you have one. After you read this book you will be faced with a choice, this choice will ultimately be on your shoulders.

Like they say in the movie, *The Matrix*....blue pill or red pill? That choice to dive into something new and exciting will lay on your shoulders. No one can make that decision for you and you must be prepared for every challenge that you will face. Change is good and I am going to give you the tools you need in this book. It will be up to you if you choose to accept them and implement them into your life!

WHO AM I?

My name is Jason Miller and I grew up in a small town on the border of Montana and North Dakota. I grew up on a farm as a hard working kid raising crops and tending livestock with my family. We were a small farm operation that just made enough to live a comfortable life. My parents worked very hard to provide for my sister and I, but it was certainly a tough road and a lot of hard work for them. We were not poor by any means, but we fell in a common category like many, we lived comfortably. There were certainly no luxury cars and fancy houses and certainly no beachfront property for a summer vacation home. But this taught me a valuable life lesson growing up.... Appreciate the things you do have.

My family has a long bloodline of military service and has served in many of the wars we have fought. Following a time honored tradition, I joined the military at the ripe age of 17 and shipped off for basic training upon graduation from high school.

Upon completion of all my training as a new Infantryman I was assigned to my first duty station. I spent the first part of my career in a light Infantry Recon Platoon as a Scout Sniper and Spotter. I have made many moves over the course of my 20+ year career in the military. I have seen many things and have been to many places both good and bad just like many of my fellow brothers and sisters at arms.

Then my life changed. I met my beautiful wife Erika who was also in the military. We instantly related being in the military and because of our common goals and desires for a future of personal, professional and financial independence. We moved from place to place as we all do in the military and realized that there has to be more.

After my wife got out of the military she found it very difficult to start a career. She would just begin to climb the ladder of success just in time for us to make that next move to another duty station. So she did what many military spouses do and went to college. She now has two Masters Degrees, but has never fully been able to utilize her education because of moving every 3-4 years. Like many, she has worked in jobs not careers.

My wife and I have always had that sense that there was something better out there waiting for us. We have discussed many times the possibilities of starting our own business full-time and giving up the hectic life of the military. At the time I was well over the 10-year journey of my military career so it made sense to stick it out and get my 20 year retirement.

So fast-forward to 2014 - I deployed to Afghanistan and spent some time there assisting the Afghan Army rebuild and take control of their country. It was there that I had an absolute epiphany as I was sitting on my makeshift bed inside a sweatbox plywood room that was about the size of a prison cell. This is where the initial seeds were planted in my mind to take action and start our own online business. I knew I was quickly approaching retirement and needed to figure out a plan for our next chapter in life.

So there I was on the crappy make shift bed with crappy internet service searching for opportunities to make money with an online business. I did the research but ultimately set it aside as an idea upon redeployment home.

When I returned home and settled back into normal life, Erika and I began to reengage the discussion of starting our own online business. I remembered the research I did on many business models when I was deployed, so we did more research and decided to give it a shot. This was an opportunity for me to do when I retired and also an opportunity for my wife to have a meaningful career working from home. We decided to become an unstoppable team and start our own online business.

We wanted to create a lasting income that would allow us to spend more time together as a family and not have to live the normal 9-5 lifestyle dealing with traffic day-in and day-out and having to report to a "boss." We wanted to become the CEO's of our own lives by taking our years of military experience and pouring it into a solid business model. Our goal has always been to earn a full time income online and be the <u>CEOs of our own lives</u>.

So we jumped in feet first and 100 miles an hour. We started attending business training, which was very relatable since training is second nature for us "military types." The training and business summits that we attended were easy to get through because it walked us through the initial process of setting up our online business step by step. We reached out to industry leaders for mentorship to help walk us through the things we didn't fully understand.

The one thing that set us apart was our consistent drive to succeed at anything we do. The military has deeply instilled this attribute in both of us. This has served us well in our business ventures and has helped us reach new heights in our lives.

My wife and I will never have to work "normal" employee jobs ever again. Our military careers have been a driving factor in our success because of that sheer will to succeed. Like many, I enjoyed the last 20+ years of my military career. It has been exciting, rewarding and has taken care of my family in many ways that the outside world cannot relate to.

However, we have now found a new start and a new journey down another path in our lives as successful entrepreneurs helping others find their success in life.

This journey has been filled with excitement, opportunity and the chance to open a new chapter in our lives with the freedom that we want to work from home, spend more time together as a family and experience the financial freedoms we have always desired. Now, I want to share it with you in this book, which will give you the information you need to make an educated decision on entrepreneurship avenues that are available to you.

DISCOVERING YOURSELF

Self-discovery is the key to learning new things in your life. I wrote this book in the efforts to help you go through some new self-discoveries in your own life. I know this book will open your eyes to a new world of possibilities. My intent is to give you some real world education that is not based on theory or armchair expert advice. If you pay attention to what is presented, you will discover some amazing things that you can apply in your life and take a small leap of faith. No matter what your age is there are always things to learn and grow from in life.

I hope this book will provide you with self-discoveries when it comes to seeking new and exciting challenges in your life. This book may not turn you into an expert business owner or a millionaire, but it will give you the tools, advice and tips to guide you in some new and exciting directions in your life. How you chose to use them is completely up to you. Dream big, believe in yourself and achieve greatness. We all have the potential to "Breach the Wall"... It's up to you to discover yourself and your drive in the process.

"Breaching the Wall "Warm Up"

To achieve greatness at multiple levels of your endeavors you have to have the spirit of an entrepreneur. The spirit of an entrepreneur is what will get you through the hard times when running your own business. Follow these simple tips as you get started and use them as a guide to your success. The word spirit should be your guide:

Self-sufficient and disciplined

Passionate

Integrity

Respected by others

Imagination

Tools for success

This simple guide should point you in the right direction for mindset in your business.

You must be ***self-sufficient and disciplined*** in everything you do. Whether it's setting your hours of operations as an entrepreneur or deciding how much family time you want to spend daily, be self-sufficient and disciplined with your choices. You are now accountable to yourself!

Do something that you are **passionate** about. Find your passion in life and work your business and your lifestyle around it. If you are passionate about what you do than it won't feel like work. It will be fun and you will enjoy doing it every day. You can also share your passion with your family and make it a family business like my family and I have done.

Always maintain your **integrity** in your business. It's something you can't get back. Once it's gone, it's gone. Be honest with your customers and don't be afraid to admit that you did something wrong. Mistakes happen in business, own them and move on.

Be **respected by others** in your community, with your customers, employees, family and other leaders in your field. Respect goes a long way with the people that surround you. They are the ones that will help you take your business to the next level.

Don't be afraid to have an **imagination** like a kid. Some of your best ideas will come with creative thinking and being a dreamer. No idea is too big or too small to try. Be inventive, innovative and adaptive by letting your imagination take you to new levels. The only unsuccessful idea is the one you never tried!

Always seek the best **tools** that will set you up for maximum success. Having the right tools, systems and processes in your business endeavors will allow you to make breakthroughs that you never thought possible.

Having the right mindset in your business and the SPIRIT to succeed is critical to your success. Just as important is the ability to operate as a business. You have to be the PATRIOT (The Protector) of your own business and business ventures.

Know how your business operates from start to finish. Know your products and customers on an intimate level and you will achieve greatness.

Planning with consistency

Actions that create revenue

Train, mentor and coach

Reinvent yourself often

Integrate your systems

Operate with consistency

Turn your ideas into profit

This simple guide should point you in the right direction for operating your business.

Always *plan with consistency* in your business. If you are consistent with your budget, your products, inventory and customers you will see success in your operation. Always be planning the next big thing and thinking about how you can tweak your business to net more profit.

Take *actions that create revenue* in your business. Often times entrepreneurs get tied up with doing little tasks that can easily be outsourced or completely done away with all together. Focus on revenue generating processes in your business that effect your bottom line in a positive way. Do this every single day!

Be the leader and *train, mentor and coach*. This could be employees that work for you or your customers that you serve. Step up and be the professional leader that you are.

The world will not brand you as a leader or an expert. You just have to own it and become it yourself.

Always be prepared to **reinvent yourself often**. Don't get tied to a specific idea on an emotional level. If it doesn't work than scrap it and move on. Reinvent yourself again and continue to make forward progress. Don't be so stubborn and married to a failed idea that it ends up putting your business into bankruptcy.

Have systems in your business that you can **integrate** with ease. Systems are what keep you going and automation is a wonderful thing. Do your homework and ensure that the systems you use will work for your business.

Operate with consistency. A business as an entrepreneur is all about finding what works and then washing, rinsing and repeating. Find what works and then maintain the consistency required to simply repeat the success you have found over and over again.

Turn every idea you have into profit. Be a thinker and be inventive with the things that you do. Aspire to remain on the cutting edge in your field and develop new ideas that produce profit. Remember, the greatest ideas in the world have changed all of our lives. On the same note, an idea is useless without execution!

Use these two acronyms above as a road map in your business. These simple tips and strategic ways of thinking will assist you in your path to "Breaching the Wall" and taking the needed steps to your own success.

GETTING STARTED

Ok, so first thing first...how to pick a product and business model that works best for you and your interests. Let's start with the basics. Making sure there is a market for the intended home business feature is important. There is little point of setting up a home business based on a service or product that doesn't have a market that people are generally not interested in. Therefore, some time and effort should be exercised to ensure the intended elements are marketable.

Consider the importance of having a separate space that is solely used for the home business. Working within this designated space will help you focus better and also keep personal and professional boundaries in place. The mental and physical positive points to having this designated space cannot be emphasized enough.

Investing in proper equipment for the home-based business is also another important factor to consider. Lacking in this area would only end up costing you further when these interruptions add cost to the overall business entity even before substantial profits are made.

From a legal point of view, all the necessary documentation and licensing regulations and requirements should be adequately reviewed and approved before embarking on the home business venture. Nothing is worse than incurring the wrath of various governing agencies when proper procedures have not been followed.

Decide What Your Interests Are:

Starting a home-based business within the lines of your own interests is something to consider as it would be a huge contributing factor to the eventual success of the business. Deciding to do something that you are good at or interested in creates the ideal mindset that will help the business become profitable, or at its worse, keep the business afloat during difficult times. Why you might ask? Well, this is a very important motivating factor for those going into this type of business venture because there is no one to poke you to press on. So having a solid interest in what you are actually doing is what can ensure the desire to succeed always stays prevalent.

When a home business is built around your interest there is also the added advantage of you having the necessary knowledge about the choice made that will help to steer the business exercise in the right direction. Going in blind will not be an issue, and good decisions can be made simply based on the knowledge that comes from the interest in that particular area.

Also in doing something that one enjoys and likes very much, the evidence in the quality of the work being produced will be very visible. When there is a level of excitement around the business environment it cannot only be a positive element, but can also help to create the ideal work mindset and physical conditioning that dictates eventual success no matter what the challenge.

Most people who venture into a home business based on their interest have been statistically proven to be able to make a success of the endeavor. Making the experience come forth as pleasurable rather than just "work" is often what keeps you able to come up with further ideas that will also positively contribute to the innovation of the business, thus keeping it relevant and vibrant at all times.

Decide What Your Strengths Are:

Being able to identify and tap into one's strengths is a very positive and advantageous thing to be able to do. What's your best stuff...the energy one is able to harness from this is immeasurable and often is the single most important factor that contributes to the success of any endeavor undertaken.

Using these strengths to further develop one's natural skills and then leverage it to their benefit is also another advantage. You will be able to eventually downplay or repair any apparent weaknesses along the way. Traditionally, people often tend to focus on the negative elements, and in the process of this they try to make the necessary adjustments to combat this negativity. However, in doing so, there is the possibility of paying too much attention to this and forgetting to tap into the positive elements that are brought on by the thorough understanding of one's strengths.

Thus, instead of harnessing and capitalizing on one's strengths, energy is being wasted on correcting weaknesses, which will eventually cause valuable time and resources to be wasted. Capitalizing on one's strengths will bring forth the highest potential in you and offer the platforms to expand and explore further avenues to shine and be productive.

Taking the time to actually explore the various interests that excite you would be one way of specifically identifying your strengths.

This can be done in a number of ways such as thinking about what excites you, what creates the willingness to extend help even when the circumstances are deemed not likely to improve, being able to identify what sort of activity will most likely attract your interest and commitment, where and when you are most likely to contribute mentally or physically, and any other similar scenarios that would cause you to be more approachable and more likely to be contributive.

Decide On Your Financial Needs:

There are several connective reasons as to why people venture into starting up their own home-based businesses. Amongst the most popular reasons is the interest in making supplemental income. Money making intentions for starting a home-based business enterprise can be a very effective and innovative way of applying one's skills and expertise to good use, and also helps one to enjoy smaller endeavors or purchases outside their current income bracket.

For a lot of people, however, the dominant factor is not about making a supplemental income; it's about surviving or living comfortable "enough" without having to resort to things like loans, government assistance, etc.

Whatever your reasons are for starting a home business, the good news is it's customizable to any financial need if the necessary effort and commitment are there.

Once the financial need is properly identified you can effectively work towards addressing and achieving this need. The element of control is then in your hands and this can be a very important motivational tool to tap into. The control factor, which lies in your hands, will then dictate the type, style, platform, dedication levels, and any other connective elements to the revenue earning capacity of the business endeavor chosen.

This control element will also dictate what level of commitment you are willing to invest into your business and will shape and establish a desired financial need.

If the financial need identified is significant, then it's more likely that you'll be more willing to go into the home-based business with an almost unwavering dedication to ensuring its success. Having a clearly defined financial need will be instrumental in dictating the commitment levels willing to be invested in your business entity.

Decide If You Will Work Offline Or Online:

There are many options for you to choose from when venturing into the home-based business field, however, the type of business chosen will in some way create the necessity to only use selected types that are most suited to the particular choice made.

Which way do I go? Working online and working offline entails very different and often conflicting elements. Therefore, when deciding to choose either option one should be well informed of the advantages and disadvantages of both styles. The following are some points that could be enlightening:

Online businesses have the capacity to be limitless when it comes to being able to reach the target audience anywhere and everywhere. There are also no time constraints and this is of course convenient for you operating the business in one part of the world while trying to reach a customer base in another part of the world. Online businesses also do not really require expensive advertising campaigns or propaganda tactics as the various tools available on the internet can be explored and exploited to ensure optimum advertising opportunities at minimal cost or no cost at all.

In most cases, online marketing styles do not require extensive office space or a battalion of staff to go with it. A lot of the work can be done electronically, thus effectively saving time, space and manpower. This of course is another cost effective contribution to the overall business entity.

All of the above applies to the offline business in the opposite way, therefore, for some, using the offline option may not be as viable of an idea. However, the advantage to using the offline platform is the very real feel of actually operating a business. What this really means in essence is offline business owners typically have much more personal interaction with their staff and customers on a daily basis, so this added face-to-face time takes up a much more significant portion of their day.

Research Companies That Fit Your Interests and Skills:

In order to make the right choices when it comes to starting up a home business endeavor, one should first understand the market sentiments. Are there companies that fit the interest and the skill intended to be offered for services and what are the expectations? These are critical to ensuring the elements that relate to the interest and skill are well tapped into in order to bring forth optimum results.

Perhaps among the first steps to be taken would be to analyze your skills and interest and then using this to gauge the lucrative aspect and contribution of the choices made.

By doing this, ideally a match would be made to the skills and interest with the selected business endeavor for successful results. The likelihood of experiencing problems that would stall the business will be much less if there are relevant skills to be tapped into whenever the situation calls for it.

To enhance the prospects chances of attracting the attention of organizations, which would be interested in using the expertise offered by the home business entity, the individual would have to ensure the existing skills are impressive and adequate enough to suit the company's needs. Keeping up to date within the particular field will help you better assess the current market trends, and thus be able to identify areas where your particular skills would be needed and appreciated.

In an age where companies are now ready to outsource their workload, being visible in providing the relevant skills needed to a company would help you attract contracts and other work opportunities for your home business, but most importantly, establish your presence whether online or offline.

Financing For Start Up:

Capital or lack thereof is always the most dominant issue when it comes to financing startups. There are of course many sources to getting financial assistance, but most of the time it's not easy without the relevant skills to do so.

Raising capital is the most basic of all business activities, but often takes up a huge amount of time and effort, especially if the intended business is home-based in nature.

Getting the cash and raising the desired capital can be done through several legally acceptable channels and choosing any one of the many available sources would help get the business started up quickly and conveniently.

First, being able to obtain and secure financing through various monetary establishments such as banks, financial houses, and mortgage companies are some of the most common options available. However, be advised that some of these institutions can be very demanding and tedious when requesting the proper business documentation before you can learn if you are approved for such financing.

Another option to consider is your family and friends. Surprisingly, these sources have been a rather popular choice when it comes to getting help. Why, because it's less hassle in comparison to what lending institutions demand. However, ensure you have a very thorough written plan documented in order to avoid communication problems or any other difficult or uncomfortable situations that could arise from this type of an arrangement.

Choosing the right person, group, or institution to approach for financial help is important and the best type would be the one who is willing to invest without actually wanting to take an active part in the daily business operation. Ultimately, whichever financial assistance is sought, you should first ensure that all relevant preparations have been done in order to be able to address any questions and queries that the potential investor may ask.

Managing Your New Company:

There are several tried and true methods that can be successfully adopted to ensure this positive end is guaranteed. Let's discus the following elements to consider when embarking on the task of managing a new company:

Leading the company in the direction of success should be the constant dominant feature at the forefront of your decision making process. Effective leadership, even if it's to be applied to just yourself, should not be underestimated for its effectiveness. This characteristic will be the overall deciding factor in your capability of running a business entity.

Growing the business is another important element to consider right from the start of the new business endeavor.

Simply concentrating on getting the business up and running is not enough in the quest to get it to the successful platform where revenue earnings are phenomenal.

In addition, having all future business plans well outlined and ready for implementation at the right intervals is crucial, especially when time is of the essence. Planning such maneuvers only when called for would be very unwise, so being prepared for all possible eventualities is something that you must consider. This will also help to keep the new business on track as opposed to having it fall apart at the first sign of a challenge.

The general structure of the business entity should be well thought out and in place so that any positive additions can be considered without too much fuss or disturbance to the original setup. That's why within the management plans of a new company there should always be a format in place for future expansion possibilities, specifically if future business plans involve a more global spectrum.

Lastly, having a vision for the new business entity and wanting to achieve it within a desired time frame is an absolute must when developing and addressing the management of the business. Your vision and goals for the company should always be centered on your customers and their needs, which leads me to our next topic... *Knowing thy customers.*

KNOWING THY CUSTOMERS

L et's talk about being too big for your britches. Another words trying to be like a big box store. In an entre-preneurial business like online marketing it's all about getting to know your leads and customers on a personal basis.

Now, a huge box store could never do this. Why? Because they have millions and millions of customers. It's not even feasible for them to have a "relationship" with their customers.

On the other hand, this is the life blood of small home-based businesses. I like to call it pressing the flesh! You can really serve a smaller base of leads and customers if you relate to them and share your story. This is so important when it comes to running a small business of any kind. Let's discuss three main points that will really help you catapult your small business into success.

*#1 -- **Know thy Customer** --* Knowing your customer is key. It's also very important that they get to know you. You might ask, how do you do this? It's simple, you communicate with your leads and customers to make them feel comfortable with you and share your experiences. Often times our stories are all the same just different content and experience.

*#2 -- **Be liked by your customers** --* This is also important, there will always be a certain base of customers that you really resonate with the most. Not everyone is going to relate to you or even like or want what you are selling. Point being here is do things that matter for your leads and provide them value. Be approachable and likable and they will follow you. This is what turns a lead into a paying customer.

*#3 -- **Gain your customers trust and confidence** --* Always be genuine, truthful and upfront with your leads and customers. They will appreciate it. Don't try to be tricky in your marketing efforts and NEVER be misleading as to what your opportunity can provide. If you do this and can provide real results for your customers than they will trust you and want more.

These are three things that big box stores can never accomplish. They never will either. Their customer base is just way too big and it's impossible for them to get down to this macro level with their customers. However, smaller business models have every opportunity to capitalize on this very simple model.

If you do this and always put your leads and customers first than your results will inevitably be much better. You will see your average customer value skyrocket and they will keep coming back for more. If you apply this simple model in your own business your results will be much better.

Let me provide just a little more insight on how you can do this. Let's use email as an example. Emailing your leads and customers every day is absolutely necessary. Here is where most business owners go wrong with emailing their lists. They don't provide any value to their leads and customers. Providing valuable content to your leads and customers makes all the difference in your marketing efforts. This also builds the three factors I spoke about above. If you provide good actionable value your customers will get to know you, like you and trust you much faster.

Be personal in your emails. Share your struggles in your own business or your life. Provide guidance and position yourself as an expert in the field. This will quickly develop your relationship with your leads and customers and keep them coming back for more.

Effective Marketing to Build Your Customer Base

Ok, so not everyone is a boxing fan but let me tell you this, the Mayweather vs. Pacquiao fight was marketing at its very best. Did you know that this fight paid out the most to an athlete in the history of sports? The cash that was made from this fight was absolutely astounding. Why? Because of the hype leading up to the fight, the huge audience of fans and the skillful use of marketing. This is what made this fight so huge and brought in millions and millions of dollars.

So how can you do this at your level of marketing? Glad you asked! Think of your business as a smaller version of promoting the Mayweather vs Pacquiao fight. You have all the same elements in your own products or services to offer... It's just a different product right?

So I have developed a formula that my wife and I have been using for a while in our own business. This formula is very simple and easy to do from a small business perspective. Remember, your goal isn't to market at the same level of this fight. You wouldn't want to nor could you afford to as a small business. So I offer the same small techniques that we use in our own business to you. This is what has allowed us to scale our business and work with a quality base of loyal customers.

#1 -- *Build your audience* -- You can't have a successful business unless you have a loyal following. Not everyone will be a cheerleader for your business but you have to build an audience that is willing to listen to what you have to say. You're probably wondering, how the heck do I build a loyal audience? There are many ways to do this. For starters email marketing is still king, build a loyal list of subscribers and provide them with loads of value. Not just content but actual value that will contribute to something in their lives.

Second is social media. There are many avenues you can approach using social media to build a loyal audience that will continue to follow you. Some of them will become customers today and some will become customers in six months. The point here is you build that audience on social media platforms like Facebook, Instagram, Pinterest, YouTube, etc. Once you have a loyal base of subscribers that knows, likes and trusts you they will be more open to purchasing the products or services that you sell.

#2 -- *Engage with your audience* -- This is the part that 98% of marketers online fail at and they fail miserably. Let's look at email marketing for example. Many marketers seem to think they can simply set up an autoresponder, put in a bunch of pre-written messages and make millions. This just isn't the case. Yes, you want to use an autoresponder but you want to engage your audience with broadcasts on a frequent basis. Share what's going on, what are you working on in your business, how can you help them, address your struggles in your business.

This is the very personal engagement that many market-ers are missing. Second, reply back to your leads in a timely fashion. These leads are future customers, if they have a question than answer it right away. If you're not doing this you are leaving money on the table. Poor service correlates directly to your monthly income! My wife and I take the time to personally interact with every single customer and lead that has a question within 12 hours! Do this and you will watch your income grow exponentially!

***#3 -- Convert your audience* --** Now you need to convert your leads into customers or your customers into reoccurring buyers. Do this by always being on the ball in your business. Answer questions over email or the phone in a timely manner. This will make your lead or current customer feel comfortable with their buying decision. This doesn't mean you have to be a sales person. It's just a conversation. If you approach it this way you will find that it is much easier to convert your leads into sales much faster. I refer to this as soft selling.

You have a conversation and let your prospect talk themselves into the reason they need your product or service. You don't need scripts or sales training. Just be yourself, talk to them like a friend and discuss some of the benefits for them if they buy your product. My wife and I have found this to work very well over the years and ditched the "sales pitch" long ago!

So these are some fundamental things you can apply in your business immediately. Like the Nike commercials always say, "JUST DO IT". You are your own worst enemy in your business!

7 Fundamentals in Our Own Business

L et me ask you a question? Do you think Bill Gates had some pretty solid business fundamentals? Well I am sure we can all answer that question. Of course he did..... Do you think he knew them when he first started in his garage? He may have had a vision but if you would have asked him I can bet you that he never expected to reach the level he did. So why was he so successful? Was it luck? Timing? Business smarts? Well the truth is this, it was probably some of all those things however; he would have never reached the level of success that he did without a strategy and some fundamentals for his business.

In our online business, my wife and I have some very basic fundamentals. I would argue that they are very similar to Bill Gates fundamental but tweaked to an online market.

Fundamental #1: Mindset -- Mindset is very important when you are starting or already own a business. This applies to both online and offline businesses. You have to get past the "employee" mentality as I like to call it. There is no one to tell you what to do anymore and all the decisions are made by you.

If you can't shift your mindset to be self-motivated than inevitably your business will fail. It won't matter how set up for success you are or if you have the most successful business model in the world. You have to shift your mind to think like a strategic business owner. You also have to be able to make leaps and take risks in your business. This is what sets successful business owners apart. You will win sometimes and lose sometimes. If you can't wrap your mind around this concept as an entrepreneur than you should probably just stay an employee! Entrepreneurs are adaptive, cunning, deal with pressure and are self-motivated.

Fundamental #2: Content Creation -- When I talk about content creation I'm talking about emails, blog posts, videos, Facebook posts, etc. Often time's new marketers are led in the wrong direction when it comes to creating content. Many will offer the advice to "Just post something every day" this is horrible advice. Content is not about quantity, it's about quality. If you can offer your loyal herd of fans quality content at least 3 times a week they will follow you forever. Be creative with your content, have a strategy for your content and most of all BE ORIGINAL.

With the changes that google has done over the past few years it does no good to purchase pre-written PLR articles. These articles have already been posted everywhere on the internet. Google will not look at this as original content and it will actual hurt your rankings in the search engines. So be original, post good valuable and useful content at least 3 times per week and keep your audience engaged.

Fundamental #3: Lead Generation -- Lead generation is the life blood of your business. If you don't have leads coming in than you will never sell any products. This sounds very obvious but you would be surprised how many people get this wrong. It's not just about quantity leads, it's about quality leads that fit into your marketing strategy and niche.

What good does it do to try and sell a comb to a bald person? This produces non-targeted leads and will result in a lot of money spent with no result. Know your market and generate leads within that market. You should strive to produce at least 20 new leads in your business per day. Use this metric and targeted marketing and you will end up with a slot machine that never asks for money!

Fundamental #4: Follow Up and Engagement -- This is the most overlooked piece of marketing in the industry. 98% of every marketer is failing at this simple step. It is so important to build a relationship with your customer base so they get to know, like and trust you. Accomplish this through email, phone calls or Skype calls and even face to face engagement if possible. People buy people, not products. If you present yourself as a leader and have good customer service than you will have leads chasing you. This can take some time when you are new but don't wait on the industry to brand you as a leader. You will be waiting for a very long time. Brand yourself as a leader and present yourself that way in your engagements with leads and customers.

Fundamental #5: Monetization Strategy -- Do you have a monetization strategy? Have you positioned yourself to create multiple streams of income? Yet another fundamental that most people fail to capitalize on. My wife and I strive to get customers every single day. But marketing should not stop there. It's one thing to have customers, but wouldn't you like to have repeat customers that buy more expensive products. This is known as a value ladder. If you are not incorporating a high ticket program into your business than you are leaving thousands and thousands of dollars on the table.

To put it simply; would you rather sell 10,000 eBooks at $1.00 a piece or 1 high ticket program for $10,000? Kind of a no brainer right? So your marketing should always have a high ticket element in an OTO (One time offer) that then leads your customers to higher payoff products. This can all start with a $9.95 eBook, then a $50 upsell that leads into higher ticket products that can be $500 or $30,000. You may be reading this and thinking Hmmmmm. Who spends $30K on a product on the internet? It's more common than you may think! So, incorporate this simple strategy into your business and you will see your average customer value go from $9.95 to around $550.00 per customer over their lifetime.

Fundamental #6: Adding the Engine -- This is the important part. How do you incorporate all these fundamentals into your business strategy? Your business be it an LLC or Corporation is like your car. The processes, procedures and business model that you use is like the engine that drives your business every day "Your Engine". This is why franchises are so successful because they have these systems in place for you to follow. The downside to this is the cost of entry. Some franchises can cost hundreds of thousands or even millions of dollars to start up. Most aspiring entrepreneurs simply don't have the capital to fund them.

That's why the internet is so powerful because you can license other people's products and sell them for huge profits. My wife and I use this business model as the engine for our business. Having the car and the engine are two components that you simply can't live without as a business owner. Many entrepreneurs spend so much time and money going from opportunity to opportunity. I like to call it chasing shiny object syndrome! Well you can break that bad habit today and stick to one simple process and business model and stop chasing shiny objects and next best things.

Fundamental #7: Just Add Traffic -- Most marketers don't have a traffic problem, they have a strategy problem. They don't have high converting offers to sell or are selling products that have already been saturated in the market. With the business model my wife and I use it's this simple...we just add traffic! That's really it, if you have a quality sales funnel that has a high ticket back-end than you drastically increase your average customer value over their life time. You must provide this "value ladder" to your business and incorporate all of the elements that I've discussed. Follow these fundamentals and incorporate a successful business model into your efforts and you will watch your bank account grow every month!

Now, you have to put this all together in your business model to make it work. Struggling business owners are simply missing an element of this simple formula. Apply these simple things into your business and you can experience levels of growth that you never thought possible. If you don't have what my wife and I refer to as an "engine" than take some time and really research your options.

Now, knowing these 7 fundamentals and applying these to your business is crucial to your success. None of these are hard to apply in your business. None of these fundamentals are really new or a big secret. The problem most marketers have is staying focused on these fundamentals. Many online business owners miss parts of these fundamentals. This is exactly why they struggle in their business.

Getting these fundamentals strategically placed in your business will allow for growth and increase your return on investment in a big way for your business.

Being the CEO of Your Own Life

L et's just face it. You are what you call yourself. You are what you believe yourself to be. My wife, personally, as a military spouse for years, called herself just that. But somehow being JUST a military spouse didn't resonate with how important she really is in the family "Unit"

If you ask the I.R.S. what she is they will say she is the head of the household. But again, something about that term is not as majestic as it should, would, or could be.

So she has renamed herself and so should you. She and I (we), are the CEOs of our own lives. Something about that sounds much more powerful!

As Chief Executive Officer YOU make the final decisions on everything that happens, not only within your family, but within yourself. You are the final decision maker when it comes to your success and your failures, your happiness and your sadness, your loves and your hates, your ups and your downs.

NO ONE else has control over your life. Sure, others can make suggestions, but when it is all said and done, YOU CHOOSE to control your destiny.

Your spouse or your significant other may offer you an idea, but when the rubber meets the road YOU CHOOSE to listen to them or not.

My wife CHOSE to follow her dream of starting her own business as a military spouse and disabled veteran. Little did she realize that action would catapult her to where she is now; coaching military, military spouses and veterans and helping them fulfill their dreams is very rewarding! Yes, she is the CEO of her own LIFE, Master of her own dream, Driver of her own destiny, Creator of her own future; she is what her mom used to call "a shot caller." She calls HER OWN shots!

She realized that this LIFE would not last forever and that if she didn't take charge of her future, then who would? Or would she continue to drift along in the wind like seeds from a dandelion in summer, being blown whichever way OTHERS wanted her to go.

So I am asking you to please claim YOUR title. Look at the three steps below to work your way towards becoming your own CEO and resist hostile takeovers of YOURSELF from outside sources.

Follow your dream -- No matter what it takes dig deep, find out what you want, and stop at nothing to find the tools and resources to build YOUR DREAM.

Know your value -- It doesn't matter if you are a mom/dad, significant other, college student, or whatever, YOU are the CEO of your own destiny. Act like it!

Handle your business -- As CEO your number one business is YOU. Even if you are a mom, dad or have no kids and just work. You can't take care of everything and hold a job if you don't put YOURSELF first. I know this is a struggle for many, however, if you continue to work and focus on this area, it gets better. You can't continue to ignore the important things in life. Is your family important? Of course it is! But, it's time for you to hold your head up and become the CEO of your OWN Destiny!

GETTING OUTSIDE YOUR COMFORT ZONE

D o you think a guy like Warren Buffet has ever been uncomfortable in his business ventures? I wouldn't want to speak for him but I would venture to guess that he has. We all have at some point. In order to reach peak performance in any business it requires you to take leaps!

Here's a recent example from a high end $30,000.00 Mastermind that my wife and I just attended (you read that right, 30K per ticket). Taking your business to the next level has its price, but my wife and I will gladly pay it (but that's a story for another time). Here is an example from this mastermind:

One of the main strategies my wife and I have been using in our business for a long time is hosting sales webinars. We recently attended a high level mastermind where the group was asked, "who's currently using webinars in their business?" Only 4 or 5 hands went up out of about 55 attendees. Those of us that had our hands up were already making multiple 6 and even 7 figure incomes with our online businesses. So what does that tell you?

The next question of course was why they were not doing webinars, and they said things like;

"I'm not ready -- I'm still new figuring this stuff out"

"What would I teach? What would I say?"

"I don't have a clue about how to actually set a webinar up, it's too technical for me"

Most knew the webinar strategy they'd just seen had a good chance of making sales, yet they were still unwilling to actually do it. So this is where the mastermind host challenged everyone to drop the excuses, and just get a webinar done. Not over the next few weeks either, but within the next 24 hours. He had to get everyone to first commit to doing it (about 85% said they would), then create their webinar registration link and then blast it out to their lists and Facebook. The intent was to schedule the webinar for the next evening.

He challenged the group to get past those limiting beliefs. He challenged everyone to host their first webinar the following night. "But what about the slides and content, I haven't even done that yet!" one person exclaimed. He replied "Don't worry about that we'll work that out by tomorrow afternoon." People laughed, but he was dead serious.

So at 9 am the next day he asked everyone how they were feeling about hosting their first webinar that evening. Many were nervous, afraid, full of doubt, but there was also some genuine excitement about doing something far outside of their comfort zone, which would take them to the next level in their business.

Here is my point: After being in this industry, seeing both sides of the coin, I can tell you the greatest moments of discomfort have resulted in some of the biggest shifts in my wife and I's income. We have done many webinars with approximately 2,000 attendees, sometimes even more. We usually have 60 minutes to provide value and also promote our business to people that are looking for a change in their lives.

We make sales and it's always our intention to do very well. To be completely honest, we always have similar thoughts to what many of those people at the mastermind had about doing their first webinar in 24 hours. We feel like we need more time, that we are not quite ready yet (just an extra week to prepare would be huge!)

Yet we are wise enough now to recognize these thoughts are coming from a place of wanting to stay within a comfort zone and that these thoughts cannot be trusted. Not if we want to get our business to the next level. So those thoughts are getting ignored.

Now, let's talk about YOU and how all of this applies to you! When was the last time you felt truly uncomfortable? When was the last time you felt you weren't ready to do something?

If it's been too long, then I'm going to guess you have not grown professionally or personally recently. That is not a dig on you, just a simple fact. My wife and I have been there and done that and our business suffered for it. I may be wrong, but if I'm not then here's my advice; Get uncomfortable. Do those things which you know deep down would create massive results, even (especially) if you don't feel ready.

Maybe it's as simple as just getting your first business coach. Maybe it's getting to a live business summit or mastermind when you're not sure if you can afford the airline tickets. Maybe it's creating your first business (LLC or Corporation).

Whatever it is, move in the direction of what scares you because it will probably make you a lot of money once you make the leap.

DITCHING ALL THE EXCUSES

I have to talk with you about this because I don't want this to be YOU! I have seen this all too often in business and don't want to see you go through this pitfall. What I am about to say might anger a few but will be the push some need to take it to the next step!

Excuses, I hear them all the time. By far the most common excuse I hear from wannabe entrepreneurs for why they don't spend more time and money on growing a new business is this!

I don't have enough time and money, I will say it right off the bat, that's complete crap! Why? Because my wife and I started out with a $3000 loan, the will to succeed and never looked back!

Not surprising though right? I will tell you right now that this is rarely a defendable answer. Rarely is the excuse of, "not enough time or money" a legitimate response. You're probably saying, "Owe sure, your making money in your business. Easy for you to say."

Nope, I am not talking about my current situation or people in my income bracket. I am talking about your situation, and my situation back when I was just like you!

Here's the reason that, "I don't have enough time or money" is a lame excuse: When I ask a follow-up question,

"How do you spend your time each day"? Every single wannabe, without exception, has listed tasks that they should not be doing.

Tasks that should be eliminated, delegated or outsourced. Problems that have already been solved and questions that have already been answered. Within the first 90 seconds of the description of their day, I identify at least an hour or more they could reassign to growing their business. In many cases even more than a few hours! This also applies to those who have a 9-5 job!

Look at this list of problems that have already been solved and find at least 3 you can delegate, eliminate or outsource as soon as you're done reading this book.

Household chores, errands, cooking, cleaning, lawn work, home repairs, grocery shopping, dog walking, email inbox management, Facebooking for fun, appointment scheduling, invoicing, book keeping, accounting, tax preparation, filing, tweeting, copywriting, blog posting, web design, site maintenance, customer service, administrative tasks and on and on and on!!!!!!

You can probably find way more than 3 right? In my opinion, if you want to grow a business, you can't afford to be doing ANY of these $3 an hour tasks.... Period!

Ok, so that takes care of the time excuse! What about the money excuse!

Well, most of those tasks, if they can't be eliminated entirely, can be delegated or outsourced for as little as $3 an hour. If you don't believe that you can make more than $3 per hour in the hours you save by outsourcing, well, I have to question your self-confidence.

The choice is yours. Do you want to stay stuck and keep solving problems that have already been solved or do you want to invest in your future? If your future is not worth $3 per hour, I'm afraid there is no one that can help you!

If this reality check made you a touch mad, but gets you off your back side than great. These are just facts that can't be denied and you have to take action. Action takers make money and wannabe's sit on the couch eating chips, drinking soda and watching mindless reality shows on television! Then, talk to their friends about how they wish they could make money with a business venture.

Which one are you?? Action taker or a wannabe!

Our intent is to get you moving. Get yourself in the right mindset to achieve success. At the end of the day your business success depends on one person.

That's you!

THE MISSING INGREDIENTS

What's S P Missing

Before I get to the actual ingredient that most marketers are missing lets discuss the components that tie that ingredient together. First of all your marketing should be more about your audience than about the product you are trying to sell.

Second, are your systems working? When I talk about systems I mean emails, webinars, phone follow-ups and product upsells. These systems should be virtually on autopilot. If they are not than "Houston, we have a problem".

Third is to build a herd, a list of loyal subscribers. Do this with email newsletters, webinars etc. Your message should be personality driven to you and your personality. Don't try to be someone you're not! On the same note you should try to appeal to a broad base of buyers. Don't just narrow yourself to a small group of people. In the beginning when you are starting out you can borrow credibility from others to get your message across.

With all of that said, what ties all of this together? The missing ingredient in your marketing soup! That element is economics. Many marketers struggle because they put traffic first. If you put economics first than your new model looks like this.

Economics >>>>> Conversions >>>>> Traffic

It's reverse engineering your entire marketing plan. The tactical triangle still applies with the 80/20 rule but my wife and I have simply reverse engineered it in our marketing planning! If you start with economics first it will be much easier to find an offer that converts. Then find the targeted traffic to send to the offer.

Fourth, have a good website, don't think about traffic first. More traffic does not mean more sales. If you don't have a good website or offer to promote than your conversions will be almost non-existent. Traffic + conversions = Profit! Once you find the right soup than continue to track, measure and improve your marketing message.

Once you have figured this out you have to know your metrics. Knowing your numbers in your business is super important. When I ask people what their numbers are and they don't know it simply baffles me. How can you run a business without knowing your numbers? In the online business world here are some metrics that my wife and I track.

- Daily earnings per click
- Cost per click
- Weekly average earnings per click

- Cost per sale
- Daily profit and loss
- Average customer value

The most important numbers we track is our daily ROI (Return on Investment). Our second daily metric is how much can we spend to acquire a customer? If you track nothing else than track those two simple things every day. If you don't know your average customer value than there is no way to know if you are over spending with an advertising source to acquire those customers.

So if you are new, your head might be spinning right now! That's ok. Let's look at some business models that put all of this into practical use. Why do 85% of franchises succeed when 90% of self-start up businesses fail? Because these metrics are already in place and there is a system to guide you. A set of procedures that you have to follow. Many people love franchises because they are 90% cheaper in some cases to start and there is a pre-established plan in place to follow.

The downside to franchises is the same positive side. You have to follow rules, this is a big negative in my opinion because I want the freedom to make my own business choices good or bad. Franchises can be very expensive depending on the model but they do work well and most succeed.

Then there was the discovery of ecommerce and info-products on the internet. This exploded the way my wife and I could do business without the large infrastructure of a brick and mortar and employee based business model. Now you could run a business from home.

Information products or opportunity products are a huge part of our daily lives. This is a multi-billion dollar industry and continues to grow like wildfire. I will talk about this more in depth later.

So, I hope this all made sense to you and how you can apply this to your own business or apply it to a start-up business.

Choosing an Online or Brick and Mortar Business

L et's discuss some of the differences between an online and offline business. Retail vs opportunity products or digital products. A good comparison is (digital delivery) vs (Physical product with physical delivery). There are many types of products on the market and many ways they are delivered. Let's look at a few types.

- Physical products
- Digital products
- Informational products
- Mom and pop services
- Large corporations

Let me drill down into the differences between physical products and opportunity products (Info-products). So what is the difference between the two? Well, they are actually very different and also require much different processes for fulfillment.

Physical products are emotionally driven, a good example is buying an expensive car for $50k. There is logic and a specific emotion behind purchasing a car at that price point. Here is the tough part about selling physical products. Profit margins are generally less and the competition is very high. There is also a lot of overhead that comes with selling physical products. Let's look at a few examples:

- Warehouse expenses
- Employee costs
- Building expenses like rent, heat, lights, air conditioning

Those are just a few that come to mind but will chew up your profit margins in a heartbeat! It takes a lot of resources to own a business that deals with physical products. This is a contributing factor to why startup businesses that sell physical products often fail. They don't do the research and end up finding out that their business could never be profitable due to all of these expenses that they never thought about.

So let's take a look at opportunity products or informational products. These products are delivered digitally and are focused on driving a result. There is far less overhead in these products. In many cases the overhead is nonexistent with the exception of purchasing licenses to sell them. Some good examples to look at are:

- Business courses
- Make money courses
- Relationship courses
- Health and fitness courses

These are just a few examples. There are tons and tons of info-products that you can sell on the market today. So you're likely wondering how to choose an info-product to sell.

Here is some simple advice to guide your decision process. Look for a company that can provide these 4 functions:

- Training, support and solid infrastructure
- Feeder products to assist you in sales for your business
- High ticket back end monetization strategy (Value Ladder)
- Phone sales teams
- Fulfillment process and customer service in place for you

So this is what you should be looking for in your quest to start selling info-products. I ran a very lucrative and successful eBay business for many years. What I found out over time was the physical product line had simply became too competitive for price. With the advent of getting physical products direct from China in bulk it was hard to compete with huge companies to make a profit. Not to mention storage of products, customer service issues and product returns.

This is why I switched to selling info-products. They are simple to sell and have very low overhead when it comes to license rights. I can show you a company right now that licenses 4 info products right now for a few thousand dollars. Now imagine being able to sell that product and not have to worry about delivering the product, customer service, returns or phone sales. That's 90% of your business and all you have to do is focus on selling the product.

I hope you see the power in licensing products using an existing business model. You can cut your cost to about 1/8 of what it would cost you to open an offline business.

Measuring Up In a Business Venture

Let's do a fun exercise that will assist you in finding out where your business stands right now. If you don't run a business than play along! This can be a discovery process for you if you are honest with yourself about where you currently stand in your business right now.

So, how does your business measure up? Are you like a big box store or a struggling new marketer?

Let's find out, and honesty with yourself will make all the difference! Here are the rules: Answer yes or no for each question. A yes is worth 1 point and a no is worth 0 points.

Simple enough right?

Question 1: Do you have a business and marketing plan for the next 6 to 12 months?
YES or NO

Question 2: Are you creating and sharing content at least 2-3 times per week consistently?
YES or NO

Question 3: Are you adding at least 20-50 leads per day into your email list?

YES or NO

Question 4: Are you consistently acquiring new customers with your lead offer (5+ per week)
YES or NO

What is your total score?

If you scored a total of 4 points than congratulations! You have the foundation in place to create a profitable online business!

If you scored less than 4 points your business will struggle to produce profit. You must focus on those questions that you answered NO to.

If you scored 2 or less than you have lots of work to do. But at least you know exactly what to focus your energy on.

So hopefully that was a good discovery process for you to go through. It's very important to answer these questions honestly for your business. Doing this will increase your profitability and guide your business in a profitable cash flow positive direction.

Many people that read this book just need some simple advice to turn some of these simple elements into a YES. I would like to offer the below guidance to you that will assist you in this process. It's simple to do and you just have to focus and get it done!

Tip 1: Get out of your comfort zone, do the things that make you uncomfortable in your business. This could be doing videos, webinars or something as simple as putting your story out there on Facebook for all to see!

Tip 2: Always Fail Forward, no matter what happens don't ever give up on your dream. We all fail at some point in our business decisions. What matters most is how you handle that failure. Will you fail forward and continue on or fail backwards and throw your hands up and quit?

Tip 3: <u>Network with the best</u>, surround yourself with successful people. Have you ever heard of the saying "You can be guilty by association"? Well the same is true with success. Surround yourself by successful people that can mentor, guide and coach you to success. This is known as being "Successful by association". There are few business owners that become successful on their own.

Tip 4: <u>Have a long term vision and plan</u>, know where you want your business to go. Forward plan what you will do every day and stick to the plan. Outsource where needed and never deviate from the plan that you set for your business to succeed.

Tip 5: <u>Be consistent and persistent</u> in your business. Have a system in place for everything that you do every day. Do those tasks that create positive cash flow in a consistent and persistent manner. Never give up and continue to push forward every day. If you do something persistently and consistently for 90 days and it's not working than tweak your strategy and continue moving forward.

Tip 6: <u>Develop your skills of asking quality questions</u> in your business. It's great to ask your coach mentor and friends questions but have quality questions to ask. When you get that one opportunity to ask a top level CEO or successful entrepreneur a question don't waste it on something fundamental.

Tip 7: <u>Embrace your lessons "failures"</u> in your business. It's not always going to be roses, unicorns and rainbows. Embrace those times where it gets tough and you make a wrong choice. Don't continue to look back on it and rehash what you could have done differently. Learn from your lessons and move in a different direction. Just don't learn the same lesson twice!

Tip 8: <u>Be vulnerable</u> in presenting yourself and your business opportunity, products or services. Let people see you for who you are and what you truly believe in. Tell your story and share your experiences with others. Most of all be honest, real and transparent with every aspect of your business.

Tip 9: <u>Most of all HAVE FUN!!!!</u> This should be fun and exciting. Being an entrepreneur is an experience like no other. If you have fun with it and not take everything so seriously you will find that the money starts to come second. Put the customers first and enjoy what you do, it's then that the money just becomes the bonus and icing on the cake!

Discovering Your Why

You may or may not have heard this before. It's important in any business to know your "why." Why are you in business? Do you know why you started a business or do you know why you want to start one now? This is a very important question to ask yourself and also to know! Let's look at this more in depth. Here are some typical answers that I hear frequently.

- I want to make money
- Create stability in my paycheck
- More free time
- Be my own boss
- Spend more time with family and friends

So these are some of the most common answers that I get when I ask aspiring entrepreneurs why they want to start an online business. I am not saying these are not good reasons to start a business but they lack depth in my opinion. Look for more meaning than just the typical self-serving answers.

What I am always a bit disappointed with is I never get the following responses. If I do they are very seldom. These are paramount to the success of your business. Here are some examples.

- To help people
- To show someone how to realize their own dreams
- To provide quality customer service
- To help a charity
- To feel good about yourself knowing you made a difference in someone's life

It is important to note there is nothing wrong with trying to improve your own life with answers like the first set of five. Most people want this same thing if they admit it or not, but here's a little secret that can drastically change the face of your business. Think about the people <u>first</u>, and the money will come naturally.

It's important in any business to profit, that's not what I am talking about. I am talking about being a business owner that truly cares about its customers. If you do this it will show on your quarterly statements. Trust me when I tell you that it will show in a big way. If you put the customer's needs, wants, desires, pains and struggles as your most utmost priority you will find success quickly.

Make these a priority in your business and provide your customers the solutions that solve their deepest problems. When you do this you put them on a pedestal and there is no better feeling as a business owner to know that you solved someone's pains and struggles in life.

Like I said before, there is nothing wrong with having your own personal goals. You need to have those goals to take your business to the next level. Just be very careful that this does not come off the wrong way in your marketing efforts.

So I challenge you to know the "<u>why</u>" in your business. What drives you to your success? What personal goals have you set? What is your message? How are you perceived by your customers and are you truly passionate about serving their needs.

Take some time to figure this out as a business owner. Put the people first and the money will naturally come on autopilot!

The Art of Personal Branding

L et's look at a case study like Richard Branson. He is among some of the most elite of the elite in the business world and a true example of what an entrepreneur should strive for. Now you may or may not like him but that's completely insignificant. What is your brand in your business? Is it just a faceless name or title?

Let's look at what really makes your brand strong enough to stand up to the challenge. Ask yourself the following questions: What are your core strengths? What are your gifts? What are your talents and what are your attributes? These things all directly impact what your brand will look like and how it is perceived.

Each of us have unique strengths, talents and gifts that come naturally to us. It's important to push our limits and challenge ourselves to do things that may feel uncomfortable or push us into directions that we are not strong in. Let's dig deeper into this!

Effective personal branding quickly demonstrates:

- Who you are
- What you stand for

- Who you serve
- How you will serve

Let's look at some factors that contribute to figuring out effective branding. My wife and I refer to these factors as the 3 C's.

- Clarity: Be super clear on who you are and who you are not. Don't try to be someone else
- Consistency: Be consistent in your message and all of your communications with customers or potential prospects
- Constancy: Always be in front of your target market. You should constantly be showing your brand to them

You are probably reading this and wondering, "How do I do any of this stuff"? Well the answer is very simple! Be yourself and let that shine through in your branding message.

There are many ways to craft your character and make it attractive to your audience.

Let's look at some examples and elements that you can use to put this together:

- Develop your backstory. Everyone has this and it's what makes your brand relate the most
- Use parables
- Define your character flaws. People don't want to see perfect, it's unrealistic
- Polarity -- What do you stand for?

Next you have to decide what your identity is. What character does your brand best fit with? Here are some examples:

- The leader
- The adventurer or crusader
- The reporter
- The reluctant hero

We each fit into one of these identities in our character. This all directly correlates back to the beginning when speaking about your own skills, experience and specialized knowledge. Putting this all together creates your unique personal brand.

Each one of us has distinct experiences that have developed our unique skills and knowledge. Ask yourself what skills have you learned, developed and mastered. Has this in essence created your personal brand and who you are?

I challenge you to look at all of these factors that create who you are and mold them into your very own personal brand. Your brand is important and at the very core of your business. At the end of the day it's up to you to figure out how you want your brand to be perceived!

DEVELOPING WHO YOUR IDEAL CUSTOMER IS

L et's discuss target markets and ideal customers. If you take a few minutes and pay close attention to every TV commercial you will see they are targeting an ideal customer. Once you have been in this business for a while it begins to become very obvious.

When you watch an infomercial, the selling strategies are designed to target a certain market or what I like to call an ideal customer, "customer avatar". There messaging is very subtle in most cases but really digs deep into the targeted customers pains, struggles, fears, wants or desires and provides a solution. This is why infomercials have been so successful. So let's dig deeper into the nuts and bolts of this.

Your leads, visitors and customers have one primary question. Do you know what it is? The primary question is, "What's in it for me"? If you can answer that question in a satisfying manner than you're going to make sales, but you have to understand the difference between your broad market category and specific target market niches. I will focus on internet marketing (home business niche) for this example. If you want to target a different niche, you would create a new and relevant lead generation (and product offer) strategy.

Here is the important part. Before you can create a marketing message you must know *who* you are speaking to and *where* they are at in the customer awareness process. If you are not familiar with this process you can see it below.

Unaware >> Problem Aware >> Solution Aware >> Product Aware >> Actively Engaged
COLD >>> WARM >>> HOT

I am not going to go into depth regarding the customer awareness process, but to put it simply, every customer goes through a process or decision point before they make a purchase. Unaware being a completely cold lead and actively engaged meaning they have their credit card in hand ready to make a purchase.

I want to focus on helping you identify who your ideal customer is. I will provide you a guide to follow to help you identify this ideal customer or customer avatar.

- Make a list of all the challenges, problems and obstacles a customer may have that fits to your product. What are their pains? Identify at least 10 "High Stakes" problems.

- What is their primary question they would want an answer to?

- Where do they hang out online? What forums? What Facebook Groups?

- How will you attract this ideal customer? List out some solutions to solve their problems.

- How are you going to serve them and help them reach their specific goals and desires?

Answer these questions and you are well on your way to defining your ideal customer. Remember the goal is to know and understand your customers to the point where the product sells itself to them!

This strategy allows you to really connect with your customers in a unique way and a way like no other. Most of your customers won't even realize that they are being "sold" on your product or service, it's completely subconscious. They will feel like it's a recommendation from a friend or family member or a well-known and trusted leader.

Think of it this way, when you go to the doctor and they recommend a prescription for an illness do you question that? I would say in most cases the answer is no. Why? Because they are the expert in their field and know what they are talking about.

So before you do any marketing, any ad copy or headlines, you need to identify who this ideal customer is. This will allow you to communicate the benefits of your product more effectively to that ideal customer. So let's put this all into action! Use the below as your guide to pinpoint and define your ideal customer.

- What is the gender and approximate age of your customer?
- What are their top challenges, frustrations, pains and problems?
- What is their WHY? What really motivates and inspires them to take action?
- What are their desires, dreams, goals and aspirations?
- Do they have any enemies? Who are those people that drive them crazy?

- Do they have any heroes? Who inspires them? Who do they admire?
- Do they have any interests or hobbies?
- Do they have any fears? What are they? Do they have regrets in their lives?
- Is anyone making them feel guilty? Who do they feel like they are failing and disappointing?

Now ask yourself, what does my product, business, service or opportunity really solve? Then list the ways your customer's life (lifestyle, finances, relationships, day to day life, self-worth etc.) will be different due to your product or service.

Once you have done this and identified who your ideal customer is than its time to shape your advertising message. Come up with a good solid headline that targets this customer avatar. Then target the main body of your message to fit the needs, wants and desires of your target customer.

Branding Yourself with Video

Earlier in this book I talked about the importance of your brand. Let's take this a bit further and move into video branding. This scares the heck out of a lot of people. It's an uncomfortable and unnatural feeling for many people to be in front of a camera. Here is the truth, you have to get over this fear and overcome the desire to stay in a place of comfort.

Your branding video will showcase who you are and what you represent to the world. This video can be a professional video or a simple video shot on an iPhone. The way your video appears to your audience is important, but the content is what really draws followers. So let's look at an outline of what your "Rock Star" video will contain from a content standpoint:

- Introduction
- Background
- Introduce your character (share something personal, dreams, goals, vision, desire)
- What was the "wall" for you?
- Stack up the problems

- Introduce the discovery you made
- Describe the unique solution
- Talk about the shift. What changed and what did you realize?
- Add the conspiracy theory, it's not my/your fault
- Highlight your success or the success of others
- Share the hidden benefits
- Call to Action / Invitation

So there is a pretty simple outline for you to follow to create your very own branding video. But let's dig a bit deeper so you have a good knowledge base on how to get started making your first video.

First, you want to capture your story in an introduction. What is your background and education? What was your life like growing up? Captivate your viewers by telling your unique story. We all have one that relates to an audience.

How did you find this opportunity, product, service, business or solution? What were your unique circumstances that led you to your decision? Get personal here and really share why you made your decision to use this product, opportunity or service.

What got you excited and pumped up about this product, opportunity or service? What potential did you identify and what got you motivated the most to pursue this opportunity that you are trying to pass on to your herd of followers. Why did you start in the first place?

Next you want to really capture your story, recall memories that contributed to your success. What challenges did you face and how did you overcome those challenges. What epiphany did you have through your discovery process?

Can you think of any specific time in this process where you discovered specific skillsets that you didn't know you had? Describe how they improved your business, your lifestyle etc. What was that skillset and how did it improve these areas. Think of some other crazy, weird or relatable story to tie in. They may not directly correlate but they can be used as metaphors, illustrations or teachings.

Now you craft your personal branding story and your offer. So you might be thinking, how can I capture my prospects attention and keep it long enough to communicate my story, build trust, rapport and sell my offer?

You can use what I call, "open loop story telling" when crafting your sales funnel. Think about one of the challenges you listed from the above questions. Where did this take place (i.e. place, time of year, time of day, weather etc.)? What was your state of mind? Really describe those emotions you were feeling as you were going through that specific challenge.

Think about that moment and identify when your emotions were the highest. What was going through your mind? Then fast forward to when you overcame this specific challenge or struggle. What event or experience occurred where you really knew you had overcame that struggle. How did that make you feel? (Go into detail and really paint this picture).

If you follow this simple guideline that I have laid out you will retain your prospects attention far longer. Studies show that you have 30 seconds to engage your audience in video before they decide to continue watching or move on. Coming up with these short story sequences will be something you can use in product launches, promotions, your follow up sequence and your personal branding. Vivid stories will be engrained into your prospect's memory and they will continue to come back for more.

"Old School" Mindset and How It Hurts Your Future

Before I get started, I know this topic is going to anger a lot of people (In the education field)! I will say that right up front! But, I am willing to take the close minded skepticism in order to drive my point home and hopefully reach a few aspiring minds that can think "outside" the old school box.

So let me explain by started out with my own story... I was raised in a family that had no college education and barely a high school education. My parents were both entrepreneurs and ran their own businesses and did not need the "typical" education that is so often pushed onto our youth today. I did however finish high school as a B-C student but graduated college with a 3.9 GPA. I can tell you that this education did nothing for me up to this point in my life!

Here is what I do know. This is the mindset of 98% of people on this planet. Most people grow up with the mindset that they must get a college education to become successful. So that's what most people do, they graduate high school, get accepted into college, wrack up student loans and enter the work force at $30,000.00 a year. Wow.... Where do I sign up for that!!! When you hear it in those terms does it make sense to you? I mean really, does that even pass the common sense test? MOST people will never see a paycheck of more than $45,000.00 to $50,000.00 per year!

Now imagine for just one second being able to make that much money in one month. It's hard to even believe isn't it? But it's going on all around you every single day. You see, we are conditioned to believe that we have to be educated through attending college and then work for someone else. *You don't have to*! This is very old school thinking and I have noticed a pretty large shift happening over the last few years. People are starting to realize that they don't have to be a slave to a middle class workforce anymore.

If you have read anything about me and my story you will see that I was trapped in that mindset myself for years. Entrepreneurship is much more than freedom. It's an opportunity to spread your wings and fly and be independent and be your own boss. Now some of these very positive things can be negative without self-drive and discipline. It's not always pixie dust, unicorns, and rainbows!

But here is my whole point... life is too short to be trapped in the rat race. There is so much opportunity out there if you want to grab it by the horns and forge your own path.

At the end of the day it all comes down to breaking those chains and reprogramming yourself from an employee mindset to an entrepreneur mindset. If you can do this than the world is wide open to you for new experiences. All you have to do is take the first steps to get there. Once you are aware of this world that you had no idea existed, you will read this book again and shake your head and say "What Was I Thinking".

I hope this was insightful for you. I know this topic will drum up some controversy but that's ok. It's all about sharing the experience and hopefully expanding someone's mind to another opportunity in life. I encourage you to find YOUR way whatever that is and strive for excellence in whatever you do. Just remember, it's your life and you only get to live it once. It's completely up to you to make it the best life possible.

PUSHING CONTENT LIKE A BIG DOG

B lah, Blah, Blah... content, content, content. That's all we hear today is content and email marketing is king. I don't disagree with this assessment that many have proclaimed! Content marketing is without a doubt the number one marketing strategy that still works today. So why are so many people failing at it? Well, that's pretty simple actually... They have a strategy that just plain sucks to be quite honest.

Too many marketers are using content that has been spun over and over and over again. It's old and people are just not interested in it anymore. They have listened to the same blah, blah, blah, over and over again. Now don't get me wrong, it's not easy waking up every single day and sitting in front of a computer screen wracking your brain about what you want to write about. After a while your idea muscle starts to get a bit stressed out!

But I will tell you this, content marketing is an essential key ingredient in your marketing efforts. I would like to share my own content marketing strategy that has worked very well for me. So some of you that are new to marketing may ask, "What is content marketing"? In simple terms, it's a process for delivering valuable content to a group of readers that is designed to attract, acquire and engage a specific target audience. The end objective is to drive potential customers to take a specific action.

Now not all marketing content is a means to convert a prospect into a sale. If you are doing this and have this approach than this is part of the reason you are struggling. Second, if you are recycling old PLR articles over and over again than this is a big mistake. Your audience will soon realize that your number one goal is to sell them something! I have been on blogs and read articles that say the EXACT SAME THING! They are just worded differently! This is not how you want to build your business or brand. Be original and write your own copy that engages your audience.

Remember this! Your content strategy ties all of your marketing together!

- Branding and positioning -- Understand your own core message, personal brand and identity.
- Acquire website traffic -- This can be in the form of blog articles, search engines, YouTube, Facebook, Twitter, Instagram, guest posts or native ads.
- Lead generation -- Use lead magnets, giveaways, check lists, short reports, eBooks, videos, webinars, events and promotions.
- Follow-up -- email marketing, blog posts, webinars, videos and Facebook
- Conversions -- In 2009 average online buyers consumed 2-3 pieces of content before making a purchase. Since then this number has risen exponentially to about 10 pieces of content.
- Back end sales -- Develop relationships and build loyalty with webinars and training. Just continue to pile on more value!

Let's talk a little bit about the style of your content. Your content and how you write directly correlates to your brand and who you are. I am branded to the more coach, mentor, and teach approach which works for me. But here are some other examples:

- Personality driven, story driven or like a soap opera -- These create a personal connection and a relationship. They also build trust in your audience. You make yourself an attractive character but remember that facts tell, but stories sell!
- Value always -- Solve problems and provide solutions. Be the one that answers questions. Train and educate and pre-sell your offers.
- Have good sales content -- Have a solid call to action, direct offers, good sales webinars and sales videos.

Now let's look at some different types of content you can use in your marketing.

Remember that this all ties back into your marketing strategy. Don't just write content in the dark, have a specific purpose for that content and where you want it to go. So here are some different types of content.

- Round up posts -- top 10 or top 100 Lists
- Over the top value resource posts
- Deeply personal "Soul baring" posts
- Educational or problem solving posts
- Controversial posts

- Review posts -- products services, software or courses
- Video posts or interview posts
- Blog series

So there you have it, this is a great guideline for you to follow when it comes to writing good quality content 2-3 times per week. If you are reading this and still wondering what to write or report about, here are some steps to further take to help you:

- Identify problems and solutions of your target market (also list out their questions)
- Group them into categories and themes
- Isolate categories or themes for your brand identity
- Brainstorm a master list of topics
- Let it flow to paper

Become more valuable. Research leading blogs, brands, authorities and "gurus" in your niche and find out what the most popular articles, blog posts and videos are.

Make discoveries. Attend, study and invest in yourself. Attend webinars, pick up courses, books, events and mastermind groups.

Putting all of this together may sound very complicated. The fact is this, it's really not rocket science. It just takes some thought process! You have to put that brain muscle that is attached to your spine to work and get the idea juices flowing.

Spending 15K for Access

So you probably read that headline and are thinking, "you're completely nuts." Who in their right mind would pay 15k to attend a business summit? Let me tell you how business really works. You have to invest in your business and be willing to take actions that grow your business in large leaps. So let me share this quick story with you.

In January of 2015, I spent almost $15,000.00 to attend a mastermind on the small island of Curacao. There was only one speaker at this event that I was super pumped to gain access to and pick his brain. If you are familiar with the TV show Shark Tank than you will know who I am talking about. His name is Kevin Harrington and he is a multi-billionaire and founder of "As Seen on TV."

So why would I pay that much money just to see someone speak? Because the information they provide is of great value. This also gave me the opportunity to corner him and pull out a few extra golden nuggets for our business. When the opportunity presented itself, I did just that. I ended up spending just under an hour discussing our business and how my wife and I could take it to new levels.

He had some great advice and is honestly just a great human being! Many have asked me if it was worth it and my answer is, yes. The ideas, concepts and mentorship that my wife and I received over that single 50 minutes of time resulted in a drastic shift in our business. We went through some exponential growth in our business extremely quickly upon returning from this business trip. It was absolutely amazing. I can comfortably say that I saw a 200% growth rate in our income in 30 days! Now, I am not telling you to go out there and drop $15k on a business mastermind!

But, ask yourself this! Would you be willing to shell out $15k on an idea like that? I can tell you that 90% of the people who read this would say NO. Why? Because they are stuck within a comfort zone in their life or their business. If you are afraid to take risks that could potentially grow a business than entrepreneurship is simply not for you! You have to get out of your normal mindset and take risks. With risk comes reward but with risk there can be failure!

That's why most people don't make these leaps. They are way too concerned about failing. I have had many failures in our business. Product launches that flopped, advertising campaigns that were duds, systems that have failed, etc. The true entrepreneur will pick themselves up, dust themselves off and forge forward.

Let's take programs for example (i.e. Affiliate programs, MLMs, Amway, Empower Network, MOBE, Pre-Paid Legal, etc.). All of these systems work, it's not the system that fails, it's the person running the business that fails. I will give you a good example... I met a guy that was involved in one of these companies. He had seen no success at all and was complaining that this particular company had ripped him off.

So I was very curious about this and ended up in a pretty deep conversation about it with him. I discovered a lot of things from that conversation. The bottom line was this, he was not following what they trained him to do. He was blindly advertising, making all the mistakes there were to make and just not paying attention to how the model worked. He didn't even attend any of the additional free training that this company offered to him.

This is how these companies end up getting a bad name.

People like this guy don't do the proper research or take the time to learn a few things and then they fail. Then they complain on every online forum they can find that they got ripped off after trying it for 20 days! This is not how any business works. If you go into anything thinking there is an easy button than you are going to be very disappointed. Running a business takes a bit of effort on your part. It doesn't matter what kind of business it is either.

So what's my point here? My point is you have to be willing to invest in yourself and your business. My wife and I have invested well over $100k into our own education by attending business masterminds, summits, conferences and so on. But with every one of these came a connection that led to another connection that led to another and another (you get the point). This has been priceless for business and has catapulted my wife and I to heights that we could have never dreamed.

Networking is such an important part of a business model. When you network with likeminded people you get ideas, advice and guidance to enhance your business. You end up reciprocating ideas that help other people enhance their business in the process, so it's a win-win situation. What goes around comes around right!

LIST BUILDING AND ITS IMPORTANCE

Have you ever heard the phrase, "The money is in the list"? If you haven't, than keep reading! If you have, well you need to keep reading too because I am going to share some little tips with you. (Your welcome).

So why is the money in your own list? Well there are many reasons for this. For starters, when you have your own list of leads you can build an audience like a mad scientist! This is so important when it comes to selling products either online or offline.

Many people are involved in the business opportunity niche or the business niche. This is the perfect place to really capitalize on your list building efforts. Many people out there use these programs as a platform to build their lists. The biggest mistake that I see is people pigeon hole themselves to one specific product or service.

It's important to monetize your email list in many directions and NOT with only one single opportunity. Here's an example. If you sign up to sell affiliate products on popular platforms like *Clickbank.com* or *JVzoo.com* there are hundreds and hundreds of options for product choices. Not to mention it's completely free to sign up as an affiliate on these sites.

You also have mid-price points of $20 to $49 products to sell for commissions.

You can also use proven paid affiliate programs and license products to cover your huge back-end sales of up to 10K per sale. But here is my point, you have to combine multiple opportunities like the ones above to monetize your list appropriately.

So how do you build a list? Now that you have some products to sell you want to start building your actual list. This requires three things.

- An autoresponder email service (recommend getresponse.com).
- Landing pages (also known as squeeze pages). I recommend the same service as the autoresponder email service since it's a one stop shop.
- A way to track your results. My wife and I use Click Magick because it's reasonably priced and has a lot of tracking options (clickmagick.com).

Up to this point I have given you every tool you need. You now have products, your autoresponder, lead capture capability and tracking services at your fingertips. Now it's time to build your list like a mad scientist.

Now you're probably wondering how to do this. There are many ways to build your list by capturing leads. I have become the masters of solo advertising. Solo advertising is nothing more than leveraging someone else's list to build your own. Then you monetize this list with your offers.

Here is where most people make a mistake when it comes to list building. You can't be scared to drop some cash to build it. Regardless of what advertising platform you use, you must be willing to invest in your business to build your list. You can do this through PPC (Pay Per Click) advertising, solo ads, PPV (Pay Per View) advertising, banner ads, blogs, article marketing, etc. That's an entire different discussion in itself.

Let's look at a simple model of how this all works and how you can build your list like crazy and offer products from the services discussed above. This is a very simple concept that does not require fancy graphs.

Traffic >>>>>>> Landing Page >>>>>>> Your Product >>>>>>> Autoresponder Follow-up

That's it! There is nothing complicated about this, but so many people are doing it wrong in their marketing. Too many people are over complicating this process when it's really very simple to set up.

The Online Magic Formula

When it comes to running your own online business, the formula for success is surprisingly simple:

- Find a popular product that people want
- Create the structure that allows people to find the products you promote
- Turn on your sales engine and count your profits

Yet while it may sound easy, executing such a strategy profitably is much more complicated. After all, if it were easy everybody would be an internet millionaire!

Finding the Right Products:

The key to finding a popular product that people will want is identifying evergreen products. These are products that never go out of demand regardless of how the economy is doing or how many people have already bought them.

These include products that either offer solutions that can never truly be solved or that feed a customer base that is continually filling up with new customers. Examples include dog obedience, weight loss, and make money products.

Internet Search Tools:

Once you have identified an evergreen niche that you will be comfortable working in, it's time to look for info-products that have the highest amount of prospective customers. To do this, you need to use the free search tools provided by the internet.

The first stop should be the Google Product Search. This free site tells you what products within your chosen niche are hot right now. In other words, it tells you the niche info-products that have the greatest number of prospective customers.

The Online Bestsellers page is another great place to find niche products with high demand. Plus, you can enroll in the online Associate's program and promote many of the products offered on the site as affiliate products on your web page(s). Then, every time somebody clicks through from your page to Online and buys that product, you make a sales commission.

Other places to look for hot products within your niche are the Alexa Internet, "What's Hot" page and eBay Pulse.

Niche Statistics for Info-products:

While Google Product Search and Online Bestsellers will tell you what info-products consumers are looking for, that only gives you half the information you need to make your decision about what info-products to promote. The next step is to compile statistical data so that you can make an informed decision.

Researching Niche Statistics Online:

You can find statistics on individual info-products within a niche by using the free Google Keyword Tool. Start by entering some generic, "product niche" terms, such as, "dog obedience training". You will then get an idea of the sort of terms and items people are searching for in that particular niche.

Sources for Niche Data:

One of the best places to find statistical data on your niche to determine its popularity is Google Trends. It will show you whether a particular niche is seasonal or whether it is an evergreen niche that has more staying power.

Using the free Google Trends tool, you can see for example that, "dog obedience training" is an evergreen niche, while searches for, "rose bouquet" tends to peak around Valentine's Day.

Determining Maximum Value:

After you have identified evergreen niches that have lots of potential customers, it's time to find individual info-products within those niches that prospective customers are anxious to buy.

To do this, you must visit websites where you can browse affiliate info-products. Some of the most popular include:

- Clickbank for digital info-products
- Commission Junction for digital info-products
- Market Health for health info-products
- Online Associates

Using the Internet's free tools to identify evergreen niches, then select products within those niches that you can promote for profit.

The Death of Multi-Level Marketing

I get questions all the time about MLM (or Multi-Level marketing) and Network Marketing. What is MLM? Well here is the dictionary definition of what Multi-Level Marketing is according to Wikipedia.org.

Multi-Level Marketing (MLM) is a marketing strategy in which the sales force is compensated not only for sales they generate, but also for the sales of the other salespeople that they recruit. This recruited sales force is referred to as the participant's "downline," and can provide multiple levels of compensation.

Now, this form of marketing is completely legal by the way! MLM often times get confused with pyramid schemes when they are NOT the same thing at all. Pyramid schemes are illegal in "most" places in the world.

I have personally never been involved in any of these types of marketing and neither should you. The risk is high and you can get into a lot of trouble by being involved. So stay away from those types of opportunities at all costs.

So let's talk about MLM. I think it's dead! MLM and network marketing is so much different than affiliate marketing. It's based off of the recruitment of others. You are always hunting family and friends, neighbors or whoever you can "convince" to join that particular opportunity.

This concept is dying or already dead. Now, those that have been in it for years to this point have an established base and are of course doing very well, but I have some friends and even established network marketers that I know that have been in this type of business for many years and they are struggling more and more every year.

Many of them are jumping ship and merging over to internet marketing as affiliate marketers. The opportunities are far more stable and they are honest and holistic in every way. So what is a good option to get started in internet marketing? Well there are many options to get started on a very low budget.

Example: If you sign up to sell affiliate products on popular platforms like *Clickbank.com* or *JVzoo.com* there are hundreds and hundreds of options for product choices. Not to mention it is completely free to sign up as an affiliate on these sites. Now you have mid-price point $20 to $49 products to sell for commissions. You can also use a proven paid affiliate program and license their products to cover your huge back-end sales of up to 10K per sale and a phone team is included at no cost to you.

These are not MLM opportunities rather affiliate marketing opportunities. You can leverage other people's products and sell them for a percentage of the final sales cost. This is a very low cost way to start up your own business. If you are interested in MLM or network marketing than this is not the option for you!

I personally prefer to sell products as an affiliate. I have very little overhead and don't have to concern myself with customer support, product fulfillment, phone sales or product creation. I simply leverage other people's products and take a cut of the final sale!

This gives you a lower cost business solution without the high cost or overhead of a traditional business. Let's face it, brick and mortar businesses are very costly and an eBay business is bulky and requires you to have physical products. Been there... done that... and also had a house full of products cluttering our garage. This is a big reason my wife and I made the switch to affiliate marketing.

Making a Hobby into a Business

Many of the world's largest companies were all started as a simple hobby. My first hobby I ever had was collecting sports memorabilia as a kid. Later in life I turned it into a very profitable business on eBay. This little hobby I had was something I enjoyed, it was fun, exciting and I had the thrill of discovering that latest limited edition piece of memorabilia.

Then I branched out to other products and built my eBay business in a massive way. This was a simple hobby that I had turned into a profitable business. I later expanded away from eBay because the competition in that market was very high and the profit margins were too low.

Here is the point, it's pretty easy to turn a current hobby into a flourishing business. Here is another example... I have a close family friend that made custom birthday cards for family and friends during their birthdays, anniversaries, holidays, etc. These cards were simply amazing. I recommended that she scale this hobby to a business and start selling these awesome cards online. The rest is history and her business is doing well and there is not much overhead in it.

This is actually how most business ventures start. There is an idea or concept, then small scale testing, word of mouth orders, and then mass production into the market. This is how you take a hobby and turn it into a business with minimal investment. Pretty cool right?

So you might be thinking.... I don't have a hobby to turn into a business. Well our answer to that is simple! Sure you do, you just don't realize it. If you don't and you want to start a business than it's important that you do something that you enjoy! That's the key here! Do something that you can have a true passion for. If it's helping people, than find an opportunity that allows you to help people. Maybe it's selling products or services! Find what it is you are most passionate about and do that one thing.

Do you know where some of the largest companies began? In their garage! Look at the computer industry for example. Microsoft began with two guys working on what is now a, "computer" from a small garage. Then Bill Gates created one of the largest companies on the planet.

So it's possible with the right desire and drive to take your hobby and turn it into a business. Sometimes it requires a small leap of faith in yourself and the courage to step outside of your comfort zone. This is what usually holds people back from launching a hobby into a business or just taking those first few steps toward starting a business.

Take the time to go through your own life and write down your ideas. What you are passionate about and what you like doing. Maybe you have this special fly fishing lure that you personally made yourself that catches trout like crazy! You can capitalize on this idea and turn it into a very successful business.

There are tons and tons of examples just like that one that people have capitalized on over the years. Look at silly putty for example, it started off as a bi-product that was used to clean walls. It was later repurposed as a child's toy and has made billions of dollars.

Our point here is this, one small idea can result in millions of dollars. Now, we're not saying you're going to be a millionaire, but the possibilities are there if you have the will and desire to make it happen.

EMAIL OR DIRECT MAIL MARKETING

Email marketing is still the king when it comes to marketing products and services. Look at a company like Bed Bath and Beyond. They do an awesome job of email marketing and promoting their product with 20% coupons for a purchase and another $10 off when you combine purchases. On and on and on right!

They are very successful doing this over email. But, they have also mastered direct mail in conjunction with email marketing. Let me use my wife as an example, she loves Bed Bath and Beyond and shops there all the time. Why? Because she gets coupons over email and gets them in the mail as well. Seems like at least twice a week, and in-store purchases except expired coupons. That's right, if you have a coupon that you received in the mail and the date expires, you can still use it at any of their stores.

But what does this do? It gives you a perceived value right? Is it a real value? Well that's for you to decide, but it's better than paying the full price right? They are reaching the online user and also the offline user and providing what is perceived to be a huge value, and it is, not saying that it isn't because if you shop there, you would be silly not to apply the discounts that they offer.

I get asked all the time about email and direct mail marketing. Most people say that direct mail is dead and it's the "old way" of doing things. If you look at the model above that I just spoke about using Bed Bath and Beyond as an example you will see that this simply is not true.

They are doing very well with both. Email marketing may be king but I would have to say that direct mail marketing done right comes in at a very close second as a way to market. Here is what scares people... COST! Direct mail is very expensive due to postage, paper and printing. So if you are going to do direct mail it's best that you do small tests with different copy to identify what works best first.

Then scale up your efforts and put more money into what is working! Now, the huge upside for email marketing is it's free. You would of course need an autoresponder service but that's really cheap or there are even free services that you can use. But the overhead is far less in email marketing vs. direct mail marketing. If you have a list of loyal subscribers you can reach out to them for virtually no cost every single day.

Here is the problem with email marketing! People are inundated with emails every single day. So what makes you stand out? You have to stand out from the crowd and offer valuable content. Just like you would with direct mail marketing. Really good email marketers know the formula to market effectively to their subscribers to turn them into cash machines.

I think it's important to optimize both avenues. Do both in your marketing and you will see a drastic change in your income from month to month, but you have to have a plan and a strategy to make it work. If you have an online based business you will have to find a way to pull those offline customers to your website or offer online. This means having an irresistible offer that your customers just have to look at. (They can't resist the temptation to see it, which drives the usual offline customer online).

If you can do this successfully than you will break into a fresh market of customers that will eventually spend their money on your products and services.

Our Simple Facebook Secret

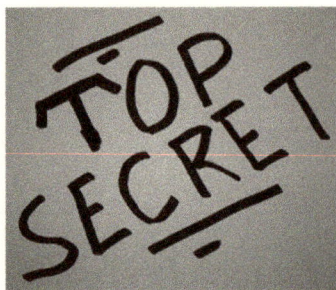

I use to absolutely hate using Facebook. I was part of the Facebook resistance for years and didn't even have a Facebook account. I did mostly traditional marketing like many others. Then, I discovered a simple and cost effective way to capitalize using Facebook to market with. It will almost seem way too simple, but it actually works. I am proof that it works and you can use this technique to build you audience and sell your products and services.

This is not a well-known way to market on Facebook either. Very few people are actually doing this and I'm going to give this little golden nugget to you for free. So take what you discover here and go apply it. Just do a small test with $5 and see what your results are!

Here is the secret formula: <u>You</u> and <u>your story</u>. So many people don't realize how much impact their story can have on other people. We all go through ups and downs in our lives, but this is what makes us relatable to groups of people.

This is such a simple concept and it works. Take about 20 minutes and outline your life on paper. Then organize it chronologically and fill in your story about your life. That's it, that's the secret! From there it's as simple as copy and paste!

Once you have written your story... This should be easy, it's your life and you should be able to put it on paper! Copy and paste this life story into a new post on your business page and run a post engagement ad for $5. You can also boost your post with your followers that have liked your page.

So do you want to know our results from the simple story about my wife and I? Well here are the results! We had 3 sales on that ad and it cost us $20 all total. We traded $20 for 3 sales that totaled just over $1,300.00! That's one heck of a return on investment isn't it!

So I would encourage you to try this very simple strategy yourself. There are not many people out there using it right now and it's a very powerful way to market your product or service. The only thing you have to do is tell your story and incorporate your product or service into it. Just tie it in with your story.

I leave my contact information on the post to include email address, phone number and how to reach my wife and I on Skype. I am giving this audience every way possible to contact me. I don't send them to a product or service to look at. Here is the ultimate goal in marketing... Stop chasing customers and let them chase you! Your story will not resonate with everyone but it will resonate with some people. Those are the people that will turn into customers for you!

So I would encourage you to try this same strategy in your own marketing. Start with a small budget and scale it up if you see results from it. If you don't know how to set up a post engagement ad in Facebook you can go to YouTube and learn how to do it for free. It's pretty simple and once you do it one time you will become a pro at it!

The Price of Scaling Your Business

I f you are new to business you may not even know what a mastermind or summit is! That's ok, I will explain it to you. Have you ever attended a live business event before? I have attended many of them to grow my business. Live events are the best way to find new business opportunities and make connections. Most importantly, make connections with like-minded people.

So in 2015 alone I attended 3 separate business masterminds. The masterminds themselves were filled with speakers that shared their business experience and gave out those precious golden nuggets of information. Most important, the masterminds gave my wife and I the ability to network with the speakers and other successful business owners at the events.

These masterminds are really priceless in my opinion. Earlier in this book I wrote about networking with Kevin Harrington who has sold billions of dollars of products on infomercials. These are the caliber of people you will get unlimited access to during masterminds like these.

I often hear people say, why would you spend $10k to attend a mastermind? That's a very simple answer. My wife and I are investing in ourselves and investing in our business to take it to new levels. These events have been critical for the growth of our business and have helped us grow our business every single month.

It only takes one simple strategy shift to take your business from making $500 a month to making $100k per month. This probably seems impossible to you and likely sounds, "to good to be true," but the fact is it's absolutely true and it can be done. You just have to open your mind up to the possibilities and lean forward.

My wife and I don't look at attending a business event or a mastermind as a cost. We look at it as an investment in our own knowledge and an investment into our business. In addition; it can be a huge tax write off as well depending on how your business is set up!

I would encourage you to look into attending a live event if you are just getting started. What you will learn there will increase your knowledge 10-fold in the business world. Now you don't have to go out there and drop 10k on a mastermind right away if you are just getting started. There are many smaller seminars held around the world that are less expensive or even free to attend.

I am very serious about my business and am willing to make these types of investments into ourselves and our business. I would suggest if you are just getting started or have been around for a while to consider this as an option to take your business to the next level. The benefits will far outweigh the costs and you will make some amazing progress much faster in your business.

If you make a small commitment to a free business event you will start to experience success in your business ventures. Attend free events, meet like-minded people, and make connections which will inevitably result in doing joint venture (JV) deals in your business.

FINDING A PROFITABLE
BUSINESS MODEL ONLINE

What is a profitable business model and how can you identify it when you see it? This is not as hard as you might think! A good business model has some key elements that make it successful. Let's look at some of these elements:

- Solid Front end products at a low price, $7 -- $99. These are known as trip wire products that get your customers in the door.
- Back end high-ticket products are so important. These are products that can range from $499 to $30k. These can be coaching programs, event tickets, courses, etc. This is what separates the everyday marketer from the top earners in the industry.
- Follow up with front-end buyers is so important. Having a good email follow up strategy is your key to success.
- Having a really good phone sales team will skyrocket your business. Moving those front end buyers through the pipeline and selling them

higher priced products is essential in your business.
Let's look at McDonalds for example. When you
go to McDonalds and you buy a cheeseburger
what is the first thing they ask? Would you like
fries and a drink with that (upsell #1) right! Then
they may ask would you like to make this a large
order (upsell #2). Then they may ask, could we
add a desert to your order (upsell #3). This is what
increases their average customer value to over $2
per customer in profit. This is why a phone sales
team is so important! They serve the same purpose.

- The systems to track your business are also crucial
for your business. Having the ability to track
sales and track what your customers are buying is
important information for you to know.

- Having a mentor or a coach is probably one of
the most important parts of your business. This
can be a friend, business partner or someone you
are paying to coach and mentor you along in your
business. If you are paying for a mentor or a coach
you have to look at that money as an investment
and not an expense.

- Customer service will sink your business if
it's horrible. Customers put more stock in the
customer support area of your business more than
the products themselves. Having a good customer
support team will increase your customers coming
back for more. You want a team that is friendly,
supportive and deals with customer questions
quickly.

- Having a solid way to fulfill your product or service
is also important. Depending on the product this

can be an area that is extremely expensive and bulky. If you are in the info-product business like my wife and I are its way less complicated. But physical products require packaging and shipping and handling.

These are just a few of the things to look into when setting up your business. If you are looking at a brick and mortar business you will have to throw the entire employee dynamic on top of this. This makes business complicated and expensive. That's why I run an internet business! I stay away from many of the pitfalls of a brick and mortar.

You're probably thinking right now...wow, that's a lot of stuff to set up and your right, it is. It can be extremely over-whelming getting all these pieces tied together properly and the upfront costs can be massive. This is why my wife and I chose to merge into affiliate marketing.

WHAT STORY ARE YOU TELLING

Let's discuss your stories and what *you* are writing about. Why do news networks like CNN, FOX and MSNBC do so well? Because they have a good marketing team behind them and they know what sucks us into watching them.

What stories do the best? The stories that do the best are dramatic, negative and often times really sad. Why is this? Because society has conditioned us to react to negative news more than positive news. This is nothing more than a marketing strategy to get more viewers watching!

Do you watch night time drama? There is a lot of it out there. It seems as if that's all that plays on the TV anymore.... Real Housewives, Duck Dynasty, My Big Fat Life, etc. Why is the majority of society attracted to this kind of entertainment? If this applies to you, then that's a question you have to answer yourself. I like the Blacklist as a once a week nighttime drama, but I rarely watch TV. If I do, I watch the Science, Discovery, or History Channels.

Now, I am not bashing these shows at all. If you get some perceived value from it than good for you! By now you're probably wondering... What in the heck does any of this have to do with my business or marketing?

Simple, ask yourself what message you are sending out to the universe! Is your message one that is positive, inspirational and uplifting? Or is it a Debbie downer that's negative, uninspiring and a total bummer?

Why is this important? Your message or your story is what defines who you are to other people. What is your attractive character trait as a business owner? What do you want to be known for and what legacy will you leave behind. I tend to float in the middle with our marketing message. It's not dreary but it's also not all rainbows and butterflies.

There has to be elements of both when you are marketing for your business. Sometimes the truth hurts and it's better to be honest in your message than be a people pleaser because most people will see right through a fake message.

I get asked all the time, how are you successful as affiliate marketers? Quite simply, I am successful because I am honest and sincere in my message. Business is not always rays of sunshine. There are times when you just feel like throwing up your hands and saying, "I'm done". That's the honest truth, and it doesn't matter what business it is. I have talked to many offline business owners that feel the same way when they see their quarterly earnings statements.

The point is your message is so important. Your good days will shine through and so will your bad days. My wife and I have days where we talk about some pretty hard truths in business. Not completely negative, but it shows you some of the reality behind being a business owner. Like I said before, it's a balance between the flowers and sunshine, fire and stone or in other words the good and the bad.

So tailor your story and your message to address both sides. That's the real point I want to drive home here. Give it straight up and unfiltered. People appreciate this kind of message! Why? Because it's honest.

Now, occasionally my wife and I will do a post on our blog as a "testimonial" for a product or service. We will give both sides of the coin in this testimonial. Not just the good, but the bad and the ugly as well. This allows our audience to make an informed decision before they try it themselves. Honesty always rules supreme when recommending or doing a testimonial on a product or service.

I would recommend that you tailor your story to fit your audience. Your story and how you tell it is your most powerful tool in your marketing arsenal. Use these powers for good and tell your story that ties into your marketing message to gain the trust and confidence of your audience.

THE AFFILIATE MARKETING FAIRYTALE

There are many "fairy tales" circulating around out there about affiliate marketing, and is what causes businesses to look the other way when it comes to starting an affiliate program. This furthermore discourages people looking to start their very own affiliate marketing business selling other people's products for a commission.

Affiliate marketing is a very lucrative option for a business who has products as well as for partners that are interested in selling those products on a commission basis. Let's look at some of the fairy tales that are circulating around out there about affiliate marketing and how each of these fairy tales can affect you and where you want to go with your business.

Fairy Tale #1: Affiliate marketing or starting your own program is simple to run:

Well, this could not be farther from the truth. As a business owner, running your own affiliate program is not easy. It requires a lot of work on your part unless you are willing to hire an actual affiliate manager. That's more money out of your pocket, which can be a pitfall when it comes to running your own program. Many businesses get into this way too fast, so do your research first!

Now, it's a different experience for an actual affiliate. My wife and I are affiliate marketers and also run our own affiliate program for our own products. The grass is a bit greener on this side of the pasture. Despite the fairy tales of how easy being an affiliate marketer are, we would be the first to tell you that it requires patients and good old elbow grease to be successful at it. It is work, and work is a "dirty" word in marketing, but in the interest of the truth, it will require some work on your part.

Fairy Tale #2: There are only a few niches that you can be successful in as an affiliate:

This again is another complete fairy tale. You can run a successful affiliate marketing business in any niche as long as it's a good product that resonates with that niche. Let me use this example: There used to be a guy on Clickbank that sold his guide to building chicken coops. This is one of those weird niches that you "would think" would fail, right? Well this guy sold over $100k worth of downloads of this eBook. Now that's impressive!! Proves our point though that any niche can be effective if you have a product to fit what the market is looking for.

Now, it is true that the popular niches like the home business niche and the weight loss niche do very well. These are the largest niches on the market and sell billions of dollars' worth of product every year. So ask yourself, "do you think you could market a product and make a fraction of that for a part time income"? Sure you could!!

Fairy Tale #3: Affiliate marketing is dead and gone! It doesn't work anymore:

This is a complete fairy tale. Let me tell you why! I have been involved in sales for almost 10 years now and by far affiliate marketing has contributed to most of our income generation. It's not old or outdated, it's very alive and well! As long as there are products to sell there will always be affiliate marketing!

However, when Google changed their algorithms, it did have a pretty big impact on affiliate marketers. Google is just not a fan of it and they make no bones about it, but smart marketers like myself found ways around this problem and have since been able to thrive as usual! Where there is a will, there is a way!

Fairy Tale #3: A successful affiliate marketer gets the product on lots of sites:

This is actually the worst thing you can do! You will blow your budget quickly and have very few results to show for it. This is a big mistake that new affiliate marketers make. It's all about quality and far less about quantity. You have to really target your market that you are trying to reach. Would you try to sell a comb to a bald guy (no offense bald guys)! No, of course you wouldn't! So it's important to target websites and advertising platforms that can cater to the niche you are working in. Place your ads there and you will see a far better result!

THE IMPORTANCE OF
HONESTY AND INTEGRITY

This is a topic that is near and dear to my heart in our business. Honesty and integrity are so important in your business ventures and will get you a long way. I remember when I was a kid, my dad used to tell me that a hand shake and your word was better than any piece of paper with a signature on it.

Doesn't really seem this way these days does it. With all the scandals in the news and companies going bankrupt due to misappropriation of funding it seems like a dog eat dog world out there. It really disappoints me that some of these companies pray on certain groups of people and rob them of their hard earned money. It sickens me deeply and this is the reason I am overly transparent in our own business.

My grandfather used to say, "listen here boy, if you ever lose your integrity.... you're dead inside" and I believe this to be the truth. Do you remember that feeling you had as a kid when you did something wrong? That pit that entered your stomach and just made you feel sick inside. This is what I would imagine feeling every single day if my integrity was not intact.

Just be honest in your business deals folks! You will find that this will get you way farther ahead than trying to play the trickster. The universe has a way of coming to get those that try to be deceitful and take advantage of others.

Now, you're never going to make everyone happy, that's not what I am saying. If you're in any business you will at some point have a few cheerleaders gunning for you in a negative way. It just is what it is, but here is the thing, if you have nothing to hide behind, than there is no need to worry about it. For example, big companies all have their haters. For many different reasons too! Most are just senseless drama to be very honest!

So don't skate the fine line in your business or ride the razors edge -- run your business completely above board and always do your customers right. Your business will flourish if you do this very simple thing.

Here is the problem! We all go through rough spots in our businesses. That's just part of business and it's what you do during these struggling moments that will define you and your brand. Do the wrong things and you can stain your brand forever! Continue to operate with the utmost integrity and honesty and you will find that the tough time moves on fairly quickly.

My wife and I had a very good friend that we'd known for years that ended up in some pretty serious trouble because of this. I won't share the details here or what the circumstances were but at the end of the day he did two things. He compromised his integrity and his honesty with his customers and paid the price for doing so. If you think for one second that you can slide by in the grey area I will tell you that it's simply not worth it.

Take care of your customers and always go above and beyond and provide superior value to them. When you think you have provided enough value than stack on more value.

This is what creates your brand as a valuable asset in the marketplace. It also positions you as a trustworthy business and people will come to deal with you directly. Then you don't have to look for customers anymore, they simply come to you!

I know this is a bit "preachy", but it's an important element in the success of any business venture. This is one of my favorite quotes on this subject matter...

"Honesty is a person's most valuable asset. His or her good name, good reputation, and good word depend on the individual's quality of honesty. A business that operates under the principles of profound honesty is elevated within the community. It is respected and treasured. The absence of honesty is a liability to an individual or business."

James H. Merkel & Abdul Wahad Al-Falaij, *On the Art of Business.*

Think about it!!!!!

Taking Charge of Your Website Traffic

O nce visitors arrive on your page, what can you do to help them make the decisions you want them to, such as following your CTA (Call To Action)? To answer this question, you have to identify three things about your visitors:

- Why are they on your website?
- How do they make decisions?
- How can the answers to these two questions get them to follow your CTA?

The Decision-Making Quadrant:

One of the best tools for understanding how your visitors make decisions is the Decision Making Quadrant, a tool developed by website guru, Bryan Eisenberg, and was first explained in his groundbreaking book, *Always Be Testing*.

According to Eisenberg, people make decisions in two main ways: (1) fast vs. slow and (2) emotional vs. logical. The bullets below present these axes into a quadrant for looking at four different decision-making types online:

- *Fast + Logical* --- The Competitive Visitor who wants you to tell them what your offer has that is better than other options.
- *Fast +Emotional* ---- The Spontaneous Visitor who wants you to tell them why they should use your product or service.
- *Slow + Logical* --- The Methodical Visitor who wants you to tell them how your product will improve their lives, along with the details behind your approach.
- *Slow + Emotional* --- The Humanistic Visitor who wants you to tell them who you are so that they can make a personal connection.

Which Does Your Webpage Attract?

Look at your existing website and identify which of these four decision-making types it appeals to the most, and which it appeals to the least. What about the other two styles? When those visitors arrive on your page, are they finding what they are looking for?

The Decision Making Quadrant can help you understand your website's current frame of reference, identify its weaknesses and help you make the adjustments necessary so that all four types of visitors get what they want from your page so they can follow your CTA.

Design Elements that Reflect Your Visitors:

The next step is to look at the design elements you can include that will help drive visitors toward your CTA most quickly.

Although web design can be incredibly complicated, the most successful websites share five common principles. Incorporate these onto your pages and you are practically guaranteed to see your conversions increase:

Clarity is King -- The moment a visitor arrives on your web page, their brain instantly goes to work trying to understand what they are seeing. To help facilitate this process, you need to give them the answers to these questions as quickly as possible:

- What is this site about?
- What can I do here? Is this something I want?
- What's in it for me?

Craft a compelling value proposition that tells your visitor in clear, precise terms exactly why they should buy from you instead of someone else.

Visual Appeal -- First impressions are critical. Keep layouts simple, uncluttered and with attractive images that set a positive tone to set your visitor at ease and put them in the proper frame of mind to make a buy decision.

Strong Visual Hierarchy -- Prioritize the parts of your website that are the most important (i.e. the CTA, forms, value proposition, etc.). Visual hierarchy is determined by many factors, including size, color, placement and the amount of white space surrounding a particular page element.

Keep Them Focused -- It's critical to conserve your visitors' attention at all costs. Nothing captures attention more than larger than life images, so consider including a single oversized picture of the one thing that is central to your business. Photos of people are also highly effective at keeping visitors engaged. A third focus tool is presenting contrast (i.e. before and after, then and now, etc.).

Limit Focus to One Action per Screen -- This goes back to not confusing or distracting your visitor. Don't bombard them with too many images or overwhelm them with content.

Boil down your website to the one action you want your visitors to take -- an image, a block of copy, an opt-in box, or whatever it is that most clearly defines what you want them to do --- then build the rest of your page around that.

OUT OF CONTROL CONTENT MARKETING

Sometimes I think people tend to overthink their sales pitch. Often the best solution is the simplest.
For example:

- 60% of small business websites don't put their phone number on their home page
- 75% don't have an email address or a link on the front page of their website
- 66% fail to put a contact form on their website so visitors can ask questions, leave comments or request more information

If your website doesn't offer the simplest things your visitors are looking for, then of course it's going to fail.

A Real World Example:

Consider Verve Medical Cosmetics, a small New York-based medical practice whose website was consistently ranking high, but was failing to capture as many of its visitors as it should.
One simple tweak -- putting their phone number in the top right corner of their homepage with the message, "Call Us"

-- and their calls increased 54%, their social media referrals increased 44% and their conversions substantially improved.

Including things like your phone number, email address, contact information, and other trust-building elements are some of the simplest and most effective ways to create a personal connection with your page visitors.

Four Things Your Website Must Have:

Look at your current website. Does it contain these four ways to improve conversions with content?

- Your business' phone number, email address and/or contact information
- A way for visitors to ask questions, leave comments or otherwise interact with your business
- Easy ways for visitors to give your business social approval signals such as Facebook "Likes," Google+ "+1's" or other ways to recommend you to their social media contacts
- Testimonials, awards, security logos, privacy policies and other content that provides social proof that your business is trustworthy and safe.

More Conversions, More Customers, More Profits:

The optimal layout is a laser-focused CTA with appealing images that grab the visitor's attention and hold onto it (*and remember to include the simple things that many small business websites forget). However, you can still fail to consistently convert visitors into customers if your site's readability is not great.

Fortunately, improving readability is one of the easiest fixes:

- Use large font sizes -- The larger the font size, the easier it will be for visitors to read, especially if they are viewing your web page on a laptop, tablet or mobile device. Text should be in at least 14 to 16 point, or even larger if you have the space.

- Consider line height -- The space between lines of text is important. If it's too cramped, it's going to be difficult to read. Set your line height at 24 point.

- Contrast -- The contrast between your text and the background can determine whether your copy is easy to read or next to impossible to see. Black on white is the starkest contrast. If you are using a colored background, be sure to choose a color for your text that provides easy visual contrast.

- Narrow Lines -- Narrow columns are easier to read than wide swaths of copy. When laying out your text, use newspaper-type columns whenever possible to make it more appealing to your visitors.

- Break Up Copy with Sub Headlines -- When viewers see large blocks of copy on your page, they find it exhausting and generally won't read it. But if you break up that same content into smaller paragraphs separated by sub headlines, those same visitors will happily scan your text.

- Bullet Points -- Why use a dozen words when two will do? Bullet points give the key information to your visitors as effectively as possible.

Every element of your web page is important and plays a key role in the success of your business. While landing on the Google front page is a great accomplishment, it's not enough to keep your business thriving and successful. Incorporating these techniques will help you convert your visitors into customers so you can make more sales, more revenues, and higher profits.

INNOVATIONS THAT DRIVE YOUR BUSINESS FASTER

In today's world of information and technology blogs have become a viable option to engage people and interact with others. We can share our world of ideas, interests and really connect with an audience that is interested in our content. Blogs have become so popular because they are reasonably easy to maintain. If you are a blog owner you can write short informational stories and then post them to release in a variety of different ways.

Blogs can be released every day, once a week, twice a week or on a schedule that you desire. This content can revolve around whatever the topic of interest is, such as politics, sports, education or maybe even a particular product that you are selling as an affiliate marketer.

One of the problems with blogs today is there are so many of them. There are simply thousands of new blogs published every day with similar content published. The good thing is blogging is free and can be hosted on a variety of hosting platforms. Many of these platforms have really good tools and even free templates called themes that you can use completely free. Choosing something that stands out can make your blog look well thought out and very professional looking.

Free and Profitable Way to Reach out to Your Niche Market:

Having your own blog that is packed full of useful information that also promotes your website or products is one of the most simple ways to engage and attract an audience in your specific niche market. If you always provide top quality content that is valuable on your blog you can build a solid relationship with your base of readers and point them straight back to your website with offers in that niche. This is how you effectively monetize your blog and create a solid profit stream into your business.

Audio Powerhouse -- The Podcast King:

Podcasting has also became a very powerful medium to reach a targeted niche audience. Podcasting is nothing more than an audio or video file that is recorded and released on many platforms to provide value to your base of followers. These audio or video files can be created at no cost and most new computers today have the ability to record for this medium. There are many platforms that these audio or video files can be published on for free. iTunes and YouTube are amongst the most popular platforms to use because they are free.

Once you have uploaded your Podcast you can approach your audience in many ways. You can broadcast your content to your list of loyal subscribers through autoresponder services like Getresponse or Aweber to get your message out to the masses. You can also leverage your website or your blog to gain maximum engagement with your audio or video content.

There are many similarities to a blog and a podcast. The key is quality content and creating multiple avenues of engagement to maximize a user's experience and keep them interested. If done correctly this form of marketing can assist you in connecting with your niche market and is a great way to further promote your website. Podcasts can be simple, easy to put together and content driven. There is no need to purchase expensive video cameras, voice recording software and microphones. You can keep it simple and record from an IPhone or simply use the recording software that is already built into most computers today.

The biggest difference between a blog and a podcast is the connection and engagement that is created. Blogs are just published articles where a podcast is actually you presenting the information either live or via recording. This gives your viewers the opportunity to really connect with you and your unique character on a personal and even an emotional level. This can contribute to building a successful brand in the niche market you are working in. In the earlier days of podcasts audio was the most popular medium of choice. Today, video podcasts have become more popular since they build relationships faster because the consumer can connect directly with you on video.

Put Yourself out There -- Build Your Character:

Reputation is the cornerstone to creating a business online. With the ability to search for information today it is easy to track down the good and the bad on almost anyone. Building a solid brand for your online business is no different than building a brand for a traditional offline brick and mortar business. Remember, you can bring the normal offline customer online. Be engaged and active in your community by getting out there and pressing the flesh. Look at other organizations online that are similar to yours and become part of their community. You can effectively syphon leads to your own brand this way and build your business.

Always be prepared to sell your brand when you can. Have an elevator pitch ready so you can briefly describe what it is you provide. One of the most effective ways to make connections is to offer tons of value and offer to be helpful. If you spend all your time asking for something I wouldn't expect to see a strong base of supportive followers. Put yourself out there and help someone else, give solid testimonials and offer free lead magnets that will be useful and helpful to your base. Do this and your online presents will explode and people will be open to what you are offering as a suggestion.

Always Be The Professional Character:

Be professional, courteous and helpful to anyone that you engage in your business. This applies to an online or offline business. The fact is, you never know who may end up a customer in the future. When you operate an online business a customer has to connect with you in a different way. They don't see you in a brick and mortar environment while shopping for products in your store. Your customer will only know your online character so be courteous, professional and consistent. Always offer tons of value and be as attentive to their needs as you can be.

Take a look at what communities you can become a part of online. This is where you can really position yourself as an expert or leader in your niche and build your customer base. You can build your reputation and even position yourself in positions of authority in these communities. This will build your brand and ultimately land people on your website or blog.

TODAY'S MOBILE WORLD

Mobile traffic currently accounts for about 30% of global Internet traffic at any given moment. It is reported that by 2017, people will use mobile devices more than PCs. I think we are already there because based on my own business analytics, over 50% of my site visitors are using a mobile device.

What are people doing while surfing the web on their mobile devices? Buying!

In 2012, purchases made on mobile devices totaled $6.7 billion -- that's billion with a "B" -- and topped $11.6 billion in 2014 and $31 billion by 2015.

Sadly, businesses have been slow to respond to this staggering shift in consumer buying patterns. According to Jesse Haines, group manager for Google Mobile Ads, only 21% of all major advertisers had mobile-friendly sites.

Although 66% of the top retail brands in fashion, hospitality, jewelry and other areas had mobile sites, one-third of those websites did not allow consumers to actually buy their products from their sites.

The Astonishing Power of Mobile Websites:

Those statistics are staggering. Especially when you consider that mobile websites are the easiest, fastest and most popular ways for your customers to interact with your business.

Mobile websites make it easy for the increasingly mobile consumer to make purchases. Nearly all shoppers polled by Google said they are more likely to buy a product or service if the website is optimized for mobile. 75% said that they would be much more likely to return if they have a positive experience on your mobile website.

Impact on Brick and Mortar Businesses:

It shouldn't be surprising that when people are on the go, they prefer to spend their money at businesses that are nearby, rather than driving halfway across town. That's one of the reasons 65% of people said they used their mobile device to find a nearby business to make an in-store purchase, according to Google.

This is especially critical for brick and mortar businesses that depend on local traffic for their livelihood, such as restaurants and retail stores.

Half of all people using mobile websites said they also use a GPS, Google Maps or another mapping site to find a nearby retail location, according to Nielsen. 44% said they have accessed the mobile website of retailers they usually shop.

Mobile searches for restaurants have a conversion rate of 90%, with 64% converting with the first hour after conducting their search for a restaurant's mobile website, according to xAD and Telemetrics.

The Power of Mobile Searches:

The trend toward mobility is global, not local. While about 8% of all web searches done in the U.S. are conducted from mobile devices, in Africa that figure is nearly 15% and in Asia mobile searches have increased 192.5% since 2012, according to Pingdom.

Locally, about half of all local searches are performed on mobile devices, Microsoft Tag reported. When you mention a location in a mobile ad, search result rates increase up to 200%, according to ThinkNear.

Social Media and Your Online Business:

Optimizing your Internet marketing website for use by mobile devices allows your business to tap into one of the fastest-growing and highly-targetable markets in the history of business: Social media.

Apps like Facebook, Twitter, YouTube and others allow businesses to get their messages in front of exactly the type of consumers who are most likely to buy the types of products they offer. But when these high-converting mobile customers are directed to a website that is not mobile-friendly, 60% will leave without doing anything, according to Google.

Email Applications:

While some pundits have announced the death of email, somebody needs to tell people using mobile devices. That's because about 25% of all people using mobile devices use them to read their emails, according to Return Path. This is especially true for iPad users, who have shown a 73% rise in the number of emails opened on those popular mobile devices.

That's significant because it means your mobile website should be fully integrated with email and offer such functionality as capturing email addresses, automatically responding to email requests and offering consumers pathways to your business via their email inbox.

MOBILE-OPTIMIZATION

Whether you're walking down a busy street, taking public transportation, driving to school or work, or actually sitting at your work desk, you notice something that is unison across all daily activities...everyone has their face firmly pressed into their phone or tablet and is either browsing their social media feed, texting with family or friends, or purchasing a product.

Our world has shifted from a direct to indirect form of communication with one another. This is no secret to anyone, but if you own a business like us, it's critical to your success that you take full advantage of mobile-optimizing your business site in order to reach the instant gratification, short attention span customer.

So what's the difference? Make no confusion about it...

Your online business's web page is different than your mobile-optimized website. A mobile-optimized website refers to reformatting the web page content and images in order to fit and work properly on the smaller screens of phones and tablets. This allows your customers to make quicker and easier buying decisions and interact in real-time by sharing photos, videos, or comments via social media.

The Mobile Customer Experience and Expectations:

If you blow it the first time when someone visits your website that is not mobile-optimized, than there is a very strong chance they will never return. Why? This goes back to the new age customer that has a shorter attention span and demands instant gratification. Whether it's chatting with family and friends, researching or keeping up with business transactions, browsing for pure entertainment, or purchasing products, your website must be mobile-optimized and take no more than a few seconds to upload. In other words, it needs to be able to achieve the same results a customer would expect from doing business in a normal in-person conversation.

Think about it, you've been on a website that took forever to download its images and text, right? How did you feel? Did you leave the site? Did you question the quality of the site? Did you engage with that person, business, or website a second time? If so, and you still had issues, I bet you never visited that site again. Think of it this way, your website must act like a business application on a phone or tablet. A business application allows customers to remove the personal contact, whether in person or by phone, and allows the customer to make decisions, purchases, etc. in a mobile-optimized way.

Positioning Your Business for the Future:

When you mobile-optimize your website you are taking business away from your mobile-unfriendly competitors and fostering loyalty from those with short attention spans and instant gratification needs. The best news is it won't take long for your mobile-optimized website to pay off because according to Google, the vast majority of customers now use their phones to browse the internet, make bank transactions, and most importantly, purchase products. Within just a few short years, there will be more phones than people on the globe; it's no wonder businesses must become mobile-optimized.

Advanced Affiliate Marketing:

When choosing affiliate products to promote, you want to pick products that cost more so that you make a higher commission per sale, however, in order to ensure your business is sustainable and remains profitable, you need to have a whole range of products at different price points.

Why is this so important? Because your target audience has:

- Different comfort levels of spending
- If one of your products goes belly-up, you still have dozens of other products to sell at different price points
- Customers that are able to afford all different price points can be pushed up the "value ladder," which means you are able to get them to continue buying increasingly more expensive products.

For example, in the internet marketing niche, eBooks and video courses generally cost between $10-50, which is a low price point that works for the masses. Web hosting programs generally range between $50-200, which is a mid-price point but a necessity in the industry. Then, as an advanced affiliate you need to offer high price points, which include personal 1-on-1 coaching, seminars, and big ticket affiliate products that range from $500-into the thousands.

Advanced affiliate marketers have these types of products in place, not only to diversify their product portfolio, but also so it labels them as an expert in the industry. If you are offering personal coaching and mentorship, and its quality, people are going to recognize you as a leader in the field because your customers aspire to have the same type of success.

*It's important to note that higher dollar products not only satisfy the customer who only wants the best, but it also allows you to sell less product, because you only need a few sales to earn big money. *This is where top affiliates focus their time and energy.*

Two great sources to start deciding what types of products you want to offer are ClickBank and Commission Junction. These are excellent sources because when someone clicks to buy a product, you get a commission.

These advanced affiliate marketing techniques will help you sustain a profitable affiliate business with multiple streams of income. Remember, before getting into any affiliate program, always do your research and read reviews from successful affiliates who have, "been there, done that and got the t-shirt." Start small and build from there.

PUPPY, MONKEY,
BABY ACID TRIP

My wife and I can't say we're football fanatics in our household, but most years we still sit down and watch the Super Bowl pre-game (mostly to get the recap of what we missed for the year), and of course indulge in the game, halftime show, its commercials, and probably most importantly, a good reason to eat until your heart rate skyrockets with the end result of a food coma... but anyway....I digress.

So, this year we were most interested in the commercials from purely a marketing standpoint to see what we could learn from the good, bad, and ugly.

...and in this household our jaws dropped and our faces speechless with the debut of Mountain Dew's Super Bowl 50 commercial, "Puppy Monkey Baby," for their latest energy drink.

However, like most everyone watching this acid trip of a commercial, we didn't even know what was being sold until we went back and watched it a second time. The first viewing of it was shock, awe and intrigue as we watched this awkward hybrid of a creature prancing around a living room. The second time we watched it was to see what the heck the commercial was even advertising. Anyone else have this same moment?

So, the point to this amusing story is really this:

As internet marketers, our job is to grab the reader's attention immediately -- be direct, demand and do not ask when selling a product, and be consistent in your marketing endeavors, right?

So based on what we're talked about in this book, having to go back a second time to view or read something would seem like a potential failure or even legitimate failure if what you're presenting wasn't interesting enough to go back and read/watch a second time (i.e. you just lost a prospect). Right?

However, in this case, we as internet marketers have something to learn. Although the Mountain Dew, "Puppy Monkey Baby" commercial was a "WTF" moment while 100+ million Super Bowl "goers" tuned in, it caused a trending frenzy on the internet and people couldn't help but go watch a second, third, and even fourth time because of its shock value (whether you thought it was funny, confusing, or just plain creepy) -- IT GOT YOUR ATTENTION!

As internet marketers, we have the ability to do the same thing in our own niche. Don't always expect a "LOL" moment or a positive reaction, but if you have the entrepreneur fortitude to take-in all types of feedback; even from the trolls out there that sit behind their computer and type nasty, unproductive messages you just might be looking at $$$$ if you hit the mark.

Remember, "Hitting the mark" doesn't necessarily mean positive. What it means is you've successfully grabbed a viewer's attention and caused them to REACT.

Reaction = engagement (good or bad)!

Elements of a Successful Sales Letter

So, you have your own product or even an affiliate product that you want to promote.

Now what?

Well, for starters, you've completed 50% of your task as an internet marketer.

That's the good news. The bad news (not really, but kind of) is you now need to create a sales page. I say this as "bad news" because many people feel uncomfortable, or don't know enough yet as a new internet marketer how to go about doing this.

But don't worry...it's really not that hard and can be broken down into 5 easy steps that will successfully promote your product to a highly-targeted audience.

Step 1: Define Your Sales Page:

So for newbies, let's first define what a sales page truly is. Think of a sales page as an advertisement for your product. That's really it! The good news if you're new to this element in your internet marketing business; you don't have to have a huge budget to create these. Sales pages are low-cost or even no-cost ways to attract your prospects because you can route them through your squeeze pages for example.

Most importantly, your prospective customer must feel after reading your sales letter that they need to buy your product and buy it now. In other words, when writing your ad, don't "suggest," <u>demand</u> they buy your product.

Step 2: Structure Your Sales Page:
Once prospects find your sales page, it should follow a <u>predictable</u> structure. Remember that your prospects arrived at your sales page by following a link on your squeeze page or by clicking on a URL for your product's niche.

Now, all you have to do is use the copy on your sales page to convince them to do what they already want to do in the first place. BUY!

Step 3: Write an Eye-Catching Headline:
Probably the most important element of the five is writing an eye-catching headline. Why, because this is the first opportunity you have to draw your prospect in. You will likely only have one chance at this.

Your headline should get right to the point and use <u>direct, active and emotional stirring language</u> to engage/connect with your prospect (i.e. what is it that your product is going to do to improve their lives, or why can't they live without your product).

Step 4: Create Scarcity:
Beneath your headline, you want to provide details about your product that are going to make it irresistible to your readers. In the first section, you want to set up a common problem that your prospect may have. Then, introduce your product as the <u>best and only solution</u> for that problem (i.e.

scarcity). At the end of your sales letter, incentivize your prospect to purchase your product by creating scarcity.

Examples include: telling your prospect there's only a limited number of your product available, or it's going to be unavailable in the very near future, or come up with another way to motivate your prospect to act immediately otherwise they may risk not having access to your product again.

Step 5: Offer a Bonus to Upsell to a Back-End Offer:

A great way to add value to your sales letter is to include 1-3 FREE bonuses that your customers will receive when they purchase your product. Typically, you want to mention what each bonus is worth so that later you can show how much buyers are getting for their money.

Upsells and back-end offers are secondary offers that are made after your customer already has decided to purchase your product. Usually, after they submit their payment information, they are taken to another screen where you can offer them more; usually higher priced products that are related to your original product.

Following these 5 steps guarantees two things:

- It converts visitors to customers
- It effectively communicates to your audience or customer what you are selling on a multitude of platforms via a letter.

Note: Always create an offer with a 30 or 60-day guarantee in order to remove any risk for the customer.

High-Quality Blogs

The objective of guest blogging is to reach the broadest possible audience from the biggest, most popular and most influential blogs in your niche.

If you have been blogging for a while or are a regular reader of blogs, you may already have an idea of which blogs fall into this category. What you are looking for are blogs that are "household words" in your niche subject.

For example, internet marketing is our niche and of course our audience's niche. So what kind of blogs do you think my wife and I use? Well, for starters, as leaders in the internet marketing industry we write our own content and blog about our own content to help other aspiring entrepreneurs and home-based business seekers. But, we also blog about other leading and respected experts in the field, such as Jonathan Budd, Ray Higdon, or Frank Kern to give our audience the broadest range of quality content.

Not only does this provide quality to your audience as mentioned, but it continues to build your reputation in the niche/industry and builds mutually beneficial relationships with other bloggers which you can call on for referrals or testimonials and vice versa.

We practice this regularly in our day-to-day activities. In fact, testimonials are probably one of the most under-rated activities you could be doing to help promote your business.

A good tool to help you as a new blogger is BuzzStream. They help make it easy to find other bloggers within your niche, build relationships with them, and keep track of your interactions with them. This tool also helps you organize your blog contacts any way you like, such as by topic, home country or keyword, and provides you with URLs you can follow to check out the blogs further.

Another option to help find "high value" blogs is to go to blogs within your niche that you enjoy or find useful and see if they list a "blogroll" in the margin. Many bloggers include a list of other blogs that they like on their own blog so that their fans can link to them.

If you know a blog is authoritative, has a lot of regular readers and frequently gets a lot of social approval signals, it's a good bet that the blogs they recommend have a similar status.

If this is a foreign to you and you are still very new to blogging then I recommend you use a tool called Technorati. This is a blog directory that keeps track of the biggest blogs in nearly every niche. It categorizes blogs by niche, topic and keywords and includes a simple search tool that makes it easy to quickly identify the biggest and most influential blogs within your niche.

THINKING TWITTER

Who would have thought that Twitter could be used to monetize your business? Most people think of Twitter as a way to keep in touch with friends, follow their favorite public figures, or simply be entertained and informed by the most up to the minute links to interesting articles and blogs.

But there are actually many ways to make money using your Twitter account and other social media accounts you most likely have.

One of the most effective ways is to drive traffic from your Twitter posts to free Cost-Per-Action (CPA) or opt-in pages. Unlike Facebook or Google+, Twitter doesn't have any advertising on it, which means it isn't getting spammed incessantly, thus allowing you to obtain massive amounts of clicks and conversions from your Twitter pages in ways that you couldn't with your other social media accounts.

The first thing you want to do is to figure out where you are going to send the traffic you will be getting from Twitter. What you want are CPA offers or opt-in pages that are going to cost the end user nothing. You can also send them to your squeeze page in which you promote products in popular "evergreen" niches so that you can capture their email address and use it to promote future offers later.

The reality is that you can use this system to send this inexpensive traffic anywhere you want, but your best plan is to send people to your squeeze page. I will be talking more about monetizing Twitter using Click-Per-Action (CPA) networks next.

CPA networks are a great place to start, especially as a new internet marketer to promote a multitude of offers in your business niche, and they are an easy way for you to get paid each time someone clicks on your offer.

As mentioned previously, one of the easiest ways to promote CPA offers is through social media, specifically Twitter. Why, because you don't even need to use your own Twitter account or promote these offers to your own followers if you don't want to.

It's much easier to buy sponsored Tweets from established Twitter account owners who already have thousands of followers. Genius, huh?

So your next question should be, "how do I know which CPA offers to promote?

Well, after you buy your sponsored Tweet (let's take the average going rate of $25), your next step is to find a good CPA offer by researching the estimated payout per click (EPC).

For example, let's say you find an offer from a CPA network that has an EPC of $0.10. Plus, the CPA network pays you $1.30 per email address you send them. Based on experience, this type of offer will give you an average conversion rate of 10% to 15% Click-Through Rate (CTR).

In this instance, for the $25 investment you made in your sponsored Tweet, you got 100 clicks and converted 10 of them. So you made $13, which means you lost $12, which is obviously not a desirable outcome.

But if you got 200 clicks from your sponsored Tweet, you made $26, or a profit of $1. With 300, make $39, or a profit of $14. So you can see the value of scaling up your offer, right? Depending on how many followers the person you buy the sponsored Tweet from, you can easily get 1,000 clicks as long as the offer matches the demographic of the Twitter account.

Remember, this is a great way to short-term cash, but if you want to turn it into a long-term business you need to use the same system to build a list rather than making money off CPA offers only. As always, THE MONEY IS IN THE LIST!

In the above example, instead of sending the Twitter traffic you get from your sponsored Tweet to the CPA offer, you can divert it to an opt-in page where you give away something free. Then all you need to do is buy an eBook as a Private Label Rights (PLR) product for less than say $10 so that you can use it any way you want indefinitely.

Make sense? Go give it a try and test it!

Grow Your Audience Online

So most internet marketers know that the more well-known you are in your niche the more likely your followers will trust you. It's really a no-brainer, however, the real skill to achieving this is through consistent and quality self-promotion. This is so important because although it took my wife and I countless hours when we first started to build our reputation, in the long run it will be easier for you to convince your audience to act on your product recommendation.

The follow-up question I am often asked, "well, how long is this going to take"? My answer....it depends on how consistent you are in your own self-promotion. If you consistently self-promote for several weeks and then take a few weeks off, well, that's not consistent and you will likely never build an audience. You cannot have ups and downs in this part of your business. You must always proactively engage and self-promote in order to build your brand!

I'm going to let you in on a little secret that will help you ten-fold. No expert in their field will tell you they do this all on their own. In fact, many leading experts outsource this type of work to a social media manager. Now, that doesn't mean outsourcing the content you share with your readers.

My wife and I write all our own content, unless we are promoting another leading expert's work in the field, but we have a social media manager to post, edit, etc. on the content we approve for our audience.

Make sense? Why is this key? Well, it saves you valuable time to focus on other tasks that need to get done in your business, so you are not bogged down on the $10-100 p/hour tasks, and rather, so you can focus on the $1,000 p/ hour + tasks in your business.

Now I mentioned the words, "Building Your Brand." So important, and I talked about this earlier in this book! What does this really mean? Well, for starters you need to stop thinking of yourself as just an individual and begin considering yourself as a brand that can be marketed in the same way as any leading company or "brand." Example brands in any industry include: Nike, Starbucks, and H&M.

When you think of these companies you don't think of one individual person. In fact, most of us couldn't even name the CEO of each of these companies. Why? Because they promote their companies as brands not people. This is the BEST WAY to convince people to do what you ask. Be a brand, not a person!

Think Oprah when thinking of people as brands. Oprah is the greatest example of what it is like to be a brand and not a person. You don't even need to say her last name to know who you are talking about, and when you hear her name you think power and influence of authority.

Most of us will never be Oprah, but apply this concept to your own business. Your goal is to create that same kind of brand for yourself so that when you make product recommendations or approach bloggers with a request to write a guest blog, you will be perceived in the same way as the companies and people I have mentioned.

The next best thing you can do to grow your audience is build a list of followers, and the best way to do this is through social media. Your goal needs to be on building a fan base so that you can influence the largest amount of people possible.

So anytime you create a guest blog, you are going to want to have somewhere to direct readers who enjoyed your content and who want to learn more about you. This should be both your blog and website because it gives you the most versatility to promote your brand, collect email addresses for your list, and promote your own products and services.

Ensure you provide links back to your website with every guest blog you publish so that you can constantly grow your pool of prospective customers. Lastly, use Search Engine Optimization (SEO) techniques so that they are ranked at or near the top of the Search Engine Result Pages (SERP) for your niche subject.

My Best Kept Solo Ad Marketing Secrets

B efore you can even begin to understand marketing and advertising there are a few fundamental strategy pieces that you must understand. The advertising world can be a very corrupt place in many ways. There are as many bad vendors out there serving Cost per Click (CPC) advertising as there are good ones. I am going to start this section with some basics behind marketing and my own personal success formula to solo advertising.

The Very Basics

Traffic Generation options: Targeted vs. Non-Targeted Traffic

1. **Targeted traffic** is just that, you must target the specific niche that you are working in. To do this you must find solo ad vendors that specifically cater to the niche that you are working in.

   *Success Example: There was a little girl in Colorado that was part of a Girl Scout Troop and they were having significant problems selling all their Girl Scout cookies for the year. So this little girl set out to find targeted traffic that would convert. She did her research and decided that her best option was to set up a cookie stand in front of the local medical marijuana store in her home town. The end result was amazing. She was able to sell out of all of her cookies in a matter of hours. This is an example of skillful marketing and targeting a specific traffic source that will convert. The formula for this example would look something like this: Medical Marijuana + Cookies = Profit.

2. **Non-targeted traffic** is traffic that will not convert to your offer and is very simply, traffic that is not within the niche that you are promoting.

   *Example: So let's just say we are selling combs and hair products in our business. We would not want to target a market of bald guys right (no offense bald guys)? This goes for any product or service. We wouldn't want to put a banner ad on a Victoria secrets website or a Harley Davidson website for an info-product that shared marketing secrets. That's simply the wrong audience to target and your marketing dollars would be better served flushed down the toilet!

Digging a bit deeper...

Keep in mind, when you hear the phrase, customer avatar, this is simply a detailed profile of your target customer. Once you've got one, you can use it to do things like market to and own a niche where you become "the one to go to," and hone your marketing message so it appeals to a specific someone as opposed to a generic everyone. This is how you successfully target your audience.

Free vs. Paid Traffic Methods

1. **Free traffic methods**, in my opinion, simply do not turn any kind of substantial profit. Why? Thing about it. Posting in forums, chat rooms and other free methods are futile in many ways. Many of these venues have cutoff the ability to lead people to your offers. Many of these methods result in one thing; a lot of time spent with very little to show for it. If you do not classify your time as at least $500-$1000 per hour as a business owner than you are making a very big mistake. Would you pay someone $500 an hour to post in forums and chat rooms? Of course you wouldn't, so why would you do these unproductive tasks yourself?

2. **Paid Traffic Methods**, in my opinion, are the only way to go. These methods are a sure fire result and they are relatively instant. If you were to place a solo ad, for example, it would be fulfilled within 3-7 days. Now, to be fair here, all forms of paid traffic can come with a heavy cost and risk. With any paid advertising you have the risk of a complete flop, but on the same note, you have the opportunity to capitalize on a huge success.

The key to being successful with paid traffic methods is having a 90 day plan and sticking to it. If you are not comfortable having some wins and losses than paid methods are not for you. The fact is this, you will have some advertising campaigns that do really well and others that don't.

How much can you spend to get a customer?

Customer acquisition is one of the most important parts of your business and knowing what your average customer value is. There is no secret to this, it's a simple formula that looks like this: number of customers (divided by) your profits = average customer value. This is a simple formula and easy to keep track of either daily, weekly or monthly.

Knowing this number does one simple, but important thing for you when you are advertising. This number tells you what you can spend and stay profitable. If you know that your average customer value is $200 than you can spend up to the $200 to acquire one single customer. No one wants to spend that much, but if that's what it takes, then accept it. If you have a good sales funnel in place with high converting upsells than you will do very well.

So what is a solo ad?

In simple terms, a solo ad is a marketing piece used in email marketing in order to get traffic, leads, and eventually make sales. Solo ads are email ads (i.e. a selling email through which you're promoting your offer) with basic guidelines that have proven successful for me in my business.

Click on solo provider's sales pages. Read several to get a feel for the community. Only use this link for learning purposes. It is for your convenience and not meant for recommendations: http://www.soloadsx.com.

There are over 400 vendors on this list. You don't have to read 400 pages, but rather, use the link as a tool to search for different sales pages.

Other Sources:

Do your research on different Facebook groups. You can join solo ads and adswaps, Solo Ads Secret Society, Warrior Forum: http://warriorforum.com and Udimi: http://udimi.com

It is recommended that you buy traffic from the top 5 English speaking countries, which include the United States, Canada, Australia, New Zealand, and the United Kingdom (T1, Premiere). People from these counties statistically buy the most Internet Marketing stuff. Keep in mind, most solo providers over deliver 10% to 25%.

Check for a picture or video of solo ad provider (good branding)

Read a lot of testimonials. Be aware that really high conversions (over 70% or 80%) usually refer to free offers. Testimonials should have realistic numbers. *Note: Visit http://fiverr.com and search "testimonials." You will see there are many vendors on this website that sell a testimonial for

$5. You should study their faces so you can identify solo ad vendors that are giving fake testimonials to boost their business. If you identify this than you will want to blacklist that vendor.

If a vendor does not work in your niche than move on to a different one. If you are selling a paid offer than you will want to ensure that you completely stay away from vendors that prefer free offers. Their lists are simply full of freebie seekers looking to download everything that you have for free. *They will never buy your products!*

Look for these types of statements on solo ad sales pages. These are things that you don't want when running a solo ad. If this is not specifically stated on the page than you will want to ask the vendor directly. (No exit pop-ups, no traffic exchanges, no click rotators, and no safelists). Your *unique clicks* will be from solo email traffic ONLY - Just proper solo traffic.

Things to understand about Solo Ad Vendors

- The solo vendor business is a business so you should expect good customer support.

- The main objectives of solo ad providers are to sell clicks and run your ad to fulfillment as quickly as possible. Remember, solo ad providers guarantee clicks, but they do not guarantee leads or sales, which has caused a lot of abuse in the business. For example, if you purchase 100 clicks and you only get 11 leads, they can say, "it could be your swipe copy or your lead capture page."

- Understand that a solo ad is a very unique way to generate traffic. Just because you purchase clicks for a solo ad doesn't necessarily mean you are purchasing a "real" or "proper" solo ad. A solo ad needs to be seen completely, including the subject line and the entire body. The key to a solo ad is the swipe copy (i.e. your ad) and it can be targeted if the right person sees it, is interested, clicks on the link and arrives to a capture page that is congruent with the ad. Since you are sending out a direct ad, the swipe copy is congruent with the capture page. *Remember, the prospect is interested from the swipe copy, not the capture page. This is what makes a solo ad targeted.

- Initially connect with the provider personally through Skype, the Warrior Forum, or Facebook. I prefer Skype because it's easy to complete the transaction and I also get a feel for what kind of person I am dealing with. I call it the "slicky factor." You know that feeling you get deep in your gut that tells you that something just doesn't feel right about that person.... listen to that feeling.

What to expect once you make the connection...

- The solo ad vendor is going to have questions for you. They will want to know what your offer is and if you have a "swipe," also known as your ad. They should always accept your swipe. Most will reserve the right to make changes to your copy, however, they should tell you what changes they are making before they send the ad out. Do not ever accept the answer of, "I will take care of it for you." Maintain control of your own copy. If they make suggested changes it should be up to you to approve it or not. If you don't like it than you can simply walk away. You don't have to settle for anything, there are hundreds of solo ad vendors out there that are more than willing to work with you on this.

Follow up questions to ask:

- Have you ran similar offers or my offer to your list before and if so, how many times per month have you ran it?
- What is the size of your list that you are sending my offer to?
- When can you run my solo ad and when will it be fulfilled?

Now, there are some quality questions you should ask depending on the responses you get back. For learning purposes, let's just use this crazy example:

The list size is 25,000. The solo ad vendor has ran your same offer to this list 800 times this month and they can run your ad in one day with fulfillment in 72 hours.

Do you see any issues here? You would think that this list is saturated with your offer, correct? (This is a very wild example that I'm using just to prove a point). You should ask some follow up questions in this case:

- How many new subscribers are you adding to your list every day?
- Would you segment your list to those new fresh leads on your list?

Let's say the vendor tells you they are adding 300-400 new subscribers per day to their list and they are also willing to segment to those fresh leads. Did we just turn a negative into a positive? The answer is yes! My point here is this, it's important to ask the basic questions, but more importantly, ask the quality follow up questions.

Before you get to the phone call...

So before you get to a phone call with the vendor, I want to share another missing ingredient that 95% of all marketers just don't do. They don't do their homework by researching the vendor on every social media platform. I probably disqualify two out of every three vendors I research with the above process and then with this last step, so make sure you do your homework and research the vendor.

For example, go to Facebook and search their name. Do they have a business page? Was it created last week? Is there customer interaction on the page? Depending on how you answer these questions, you can identify red flags before you even waste your time engaging with them on the phone. Repeat this process on Twitter, Instagram, Google+, LinkedIn, Pinterest, YouTube, Google, Bing and Yahoo. This will give you some background on the vendor and you will likely disqualify many of them before you ever get to the phone call phase.

*Remember, it's your money and you should protect it at all cost.

JV Rocket and "Tier 1 Solo Ads"

With JV Rocket you can buy a solo ad that will go out to a double opt-in list of 226,000+ subscribers for the price of

$2,500. Your ad goes out to customers who have purchased ClickBank products in the "make money" niche such as Get Google Ads for free, Health Biz in a Box, Forced Money, Top Secret Magic Code, and many more.

Many of the top internet marketing and "make money" niche gurus are using JV Rocket to build their lists and directly email their hot offers. $2,500 is a considerable amount of money to risk for most people, so before testing JV Rocket you'll want to make sure you have tested sales materials and a really good funnel. You'll also want to be sure that your offer is a good match for the type of customers who would buy the type of products I just mentioned above.

This doesn't mean that your offers must be similar, but it does mean that the same demographic would order your product. The downside of this solo ad source is that there are no guaranteed amount of visitors you'll get. The upside is, if you have an offer that's on fire and would work well with these type of customers, then JV Rocket can be a goldmine. Just remember, as with any of these ad sources, you're responsible for your business and the risks you take when buying advertising.

Profiting from paid advertising is simple, but not easy. Here's what I mean. It would be easy to blow through $10,000 on JV Rocket. The inventory is there waiting for you to order anytime you want. However, it would be wise to test your sales funnel out by buying solo ads on a smaller scale at $30, $100, or $300 from "Tier 2 Solo Ad" vendors such as the ones on Safe-Swaps.com, SoloAdDirectory.com, or Directory of Ezines.

After you have a tested and proven funnel that works well with the solo ads you've purchased on a small scale, then you may want to consider going big time and ordering what I call, "Tier 1 Solo Ads" using JV Rocket as your source.

When I'm actively running solo ads, I'm usually able to generate hundreds of leads per day. This may change down the road, but as of right now, solo ads are cheap, they're effective and very easy because you don't have to worry about landing page quality score, paying per click or keeping an eye on your ads and paying by the click.

Let's say you buy a solo ad for $300 for 1,000 clicks. You pay 60 cents per click and you know exactly how many clicks are going to come to your site. The vendor who sends you a solo ad sends an ad out to his/her email list, which recommends your freebie or your website. So, in essence, they are transferring their authority over to you. That's what makes it the most effective way of generating traffic, in my opinion. Since the ads are still cheap, it's very effective for anybody who has the money to risk on it.

I realize it's not going to be easy to find solo ad sellers if you have no clue about the world of solo ads right now, but once you find reputable sellers, you want to start connecting with them on Skype. Why? Because I have learned in meeting many different solo ad sellers that a lot of times they will give you great deals on Skype that they don't advertise outside of this platform. You can also find solo ads in one location called soloadddirectory.com. This is a resource I used when I was a newbie marketer.

The key to having profitable solo ads is your sales funnel. You want to have a squeeze page or lead capture page that generates leads through giving away a lead magnet. Then you have an upsell from there, which will be a one-time offer for something that's in the $17-$49 price point. Once your lead has purchased, you then want to begin offering higher price point upsells so you can afford to pay for your solo ads.

Now, you may also want to promote offers on the download page for freebies that you're giving away. That way you can come close to breaking even or you can profit directly from that solo ad before you even get the subscribers on your list. I haven't profited from many solo ads right up front, but I made a profit on the back end from promoting strictly to the subscriber list. That's something <u>you</u> must do.

Remember, a lot of companies in advertising are willing to pay a lot of money upfront and even lose money on the front end. They know they're going to make money on the backend with their follow up marketing, which is what email marketing is all about.

I hope these best kept secrets were of value to you. I've decided to go much farther with just this book and would invite you to see this very process in real time by visiting http://mysolosecret.com

On this page you will be able to watch three, 15 minute videos that walk you through how to make solo ads profitable. There is no obligation, no lead capture page, and no purchase required to attend this training. This training is strictly being offered for free to anyone that purchased this book.

CLOSING THOUGHTS

You made it to the end!! I hope this book was an enlightening tool for you. Hopefully you took away some very key concepts to help you in your current business or help you get started in your very first business. Over many years in marketing, I have been very fortunate to learn, grow and profit in this business. There is no reason why you can't find the same success that I've had.

Apply the "hustle" and marketing instincts that will allow you to profit in your business. Remember, there are three components to your success: (1) continuous education, (2) sell, sell, sell and (3) take care of your leads and customers! Find the right opportunity at the right time, get with the right people and you will find that success is abound.

Now, there is one last thing for you to consider. This component has been one of the biggest keys to my success. Having a coach, mentor, business partner or just a friend to bounce ideas off of is vital to the success of your business.

No successful entrepreneur or successful company has been built without the help of a trusted advisor, business partner, mentor or just a friend. This is important for one very simple reason. Just because you think something is a good idea doesn't mean that it is. I can recall many times when I thought I had a good idea for a new product or marketing strategy but my mentor would eventually say, "that won't work." Very irritating at times but it's good to have someone that has been there, done that in your corner. This keeps us accountable as business owners and prevents us from making very costly mistakes.

So I challenge you to put all these resources to good use and apply them in your marketing. Business loves speed and so does money. This is why you have to get off your butt and stop talking about making money and take action. If you do not like your current outcome in life than it is time to change those outcomes with a new course of action. If you implement the information from this book, work hard, remain dedicated to your business, and face challenges head on with action than you to will be able to "breach the wall" into successful entrepreneurship.

THE STRATEGIC ADVISOR BOARD

The Strategic Advisor Board is a dynamic team that partners with your business to create custom strategies to help you grow your business on multiple levels. We look at the core foundation and systems within your current business to refine approaches, establish cost-saving measures, and ensure your systems are functioning at the highest efficiency and profitability. We add value to your business to place your business in the best position to implement strategies to scale.

We help businesses emerge from the growth to scale. When a small business grows, resources are added, employees are hired to serve more clients, and strength is added to the business within operations. Scaling your business is where you reframe your brand, automate many of your practices, and create strategic partnerships to begin the process to expand your influence in the marketplace. A comprehensive strategy, a team to support your business, and a trusted network of business service providers is what the Strategic Advisor Board offers to help your business grow into an influential brand. Our multifaceted and dynamic approach to partnering to develop custom strategies to grow and scale your business is unique in the marketplace.

Are you ready to take the next step in your business?

Learn more at www.strategicadvisorboard.com.

PATRIOT COMMUNITY OUTREACH PROGRAM

Help someone that you know in need. This special card, when presented at most prescription counters, will save you up to 79% on the purchase of most prescription drugs. There is no obligation, no activation required and there are no fees to use this powerful card - just savings for the user!

In today's world of high prescription drug costs every little bit counts!

To learn more about this card, read testimonials of actual card users, download additional cards for your family and friends, and look up store locations and savings, visit our website at http://patriotsoutreach.com (This savings program is only available in the U.S.)

HELP US HELP MILLIONS OF PEOPLE TODAY!

PRINT A CARD OR GIVE ONE TO SOMEONE WHO NEEDS ONE TODAY! HELP US SAVE MILLIONS OF $$ TODAY!!

http://patriotsoutreach.com

WHAT DO A FEW OF MY STUDENTS HAVE TO SAY?

"I love that Jason is honest about business! It takes determination and patience. Jason's coaching style is down-to-earth and easy to understand to lay people. Those that are new to business will be able to implement the scenarios discussed with ease! I sent him an email not quite understanding a few things and Jason took it upon himself to call me. After our call I was able to relax and understand the process better. I really appreciate Jason for reaching out to me the way he did. I'm lucky to have such an awesome coach!!! I felt confident that I could effectively apply the strategies my coach taught me. Jason Miller is wonderful!"

"Jason Miller has been a pleasure to work with. Once I found out we had military background we hit it off. Jason has been great explaining everything from the beginning. We have worked together to where I have my autoresponder set up completely and I'm ready to start building my email list for my business. He has been great with checking over my work to make sure I'm doing it right and when I'm not he explains in detail of what I need to change and why. Awesome Coach!!

What is great is I can always send a text through Skype and he always gets back to me quickly. It's nice to know he is just a click away.

What I like about Jason is I feel we will be friends even after our coaching lessons are over with. He is just that type of a person that makes you feel like a friend. He doesn't over power you with information and makes sure you're comfortable with what you need to be doing. He makes you feel comfortable to talk to and ask those dumb questions. All I can say is I am thankful to have Jason Miller as my coach. Perfect fit!"

"Jason gets right to business AND is a great listener AND effectively moves the iceberg (me) in the right direction. It's great to know that I'm getting MAXIMUM value from every minute during my coaching sessions. Also, Jason's "no hype" approach to coaching is refreshing and effective. His ability to communicate with laser focus helps expand my vision AND confidence about my Internet business. This comes in handy when I'm spinning my wheels from information overload. Jason's mastery of skills necessary to be a coach are GREATLY APPRICIATED! Looking forward to all future sessions!"

"I have had 2 sessions with Jason Miller, plus I've gone through his training on YouTube. He is EXCELLENT. Jason is very easy to understand and very encouraging during our sessions. I was very impressed with Jason's dedication to his trainees as he was even doing coaching sessions with them on Skype while on vacation. Now that is DEDICATION!!

His willingness to talk to us on our level and coach us through our questions and problems is amazing. We are looking forward to continuing our training with him when we arrive home from our trip. Jason doesn't hold anything back when he is teaching us and we really appreciate his openness. He is an Amazing Asset to have on your side in business and definitely to me"

"Jason may have been the absolutely perfect coach selection for me. I like his instruction methods and his ability to reduce the complex to the understandable. His willingness to happily spend more than the allocated time is much appreciated by me.

Friendly, punctual, knowledgeable, disciplined in staying on topic till I fully understood the subject. Always willing to critique and advise on copy. Provided answers to questions outside of the allotted and required time allocation. All in all a true professional who tells it like it is.

With still many more sessions available to me with Jason I would have to say I am deeply impressed with the caliber and integrity of his coaching. I'm happy that Jason is my coach. I believe it's a good fit."

"I love Jason. He is clear and well spoken. He understands my level and talks to where I am at in my business. He is patient with me and answers all my questions. He works well with my learning pace and me. He often spends more than the allotted with me on the Skype. He is thorough and keeps us on the subject matter. He is understanding of where I am at and able to move at my pace. Very open and willing to help me improve. Jason is a strong individual with good skills and good with people. I am very pleased with him and glad he is my coach."

www.ingramcontent.com/pod-product-compliance
Lightning Source LLC
Chambersburg PA
CBHW031359180326
41458CB00043B/6544/J